ARISE TO CONQUER

To the ground staff of the RAF, without whose essential work the Battle of the Air could never be fought.

ARISE TO CONQUER

The 'Real' Hurricane Pilot

Wing Commander I.R. Gleed DSO, DFC
Introduced by Dilip Sarkar MBE, FRHistS

AIR WORLD

ARISE TO CONQUER
The 'Real' Hurricane Pilot

This edition published in 2022 by
Air World
An imprint of
Pen & Sword Books Ltd
Yorkshire – Philadelphia

First published by Victor Gollancz Ltd., London, 1942

Typeset by SJmagic DESIGN SERVICES, India.

Printed and bound in the UK by CPI Group (UK) Ltd.

Pen & Sword Books Ltd incorporates the imprints of Pen & Sword Archaeology, Air World Books, Atlas, Aviation, Battleground, Discovery, Family History, History, Maritime, Military, Naval, Politics, Social History, Transport, True Crime, Claymore Press, Frontline Books, Praetorian Press, Seaforth Publishing and White Owl

For a complete list of Pen & Sword titles please contact

PEN & SWORD BOOKS LIMITED
47 Church Street, Barnsley, South Yorkshire, S70 2AS, England.
E-mail: enquiries@pen-and-sword.co.uk
Website: www.pen-and-sword.co.uk

Or

PEN AND SWORD BOOKS
1950 Lawrence Rd, Havertown, PA 19083, USA
E-mail: Uspen-and-sword@casematepublishers.com
Website: www.penandswordbooks.com

Contents

Preface

During the Second World War, the public demand for accounts from combatants, and fighter pilots in particular, was insatiable. Indeed, Fighter Command's victory during the Battle of Britain in 1940 ensured that the 'Fighter Boys', especially those who flew single-engine types like the glamorous Supermarine Spitfire and Hawker Hurricane, became the stars of their day, their scores of enemy aircraft destroyed and aerial exploits eagerly followed by an adoring public.

After the Battle of Britain, several fighter 'aces', which is to say pilots who had destroyed five or more aircraft, wrote first-hand accounts of their experiences during 1940, that tumultuous year which had seen France fall, the British Expeditionary Force evacuated from Dunkirk, and the Battle of Britain. Two of these authors were Spitfire pilots, namely Flight Lieutenant David Crook DFC, who wrote *Spitfire Pilot*, and Squadron Leader Brian Lane DFC, who penned *Spitfire! The Experiences of a Fighter Pilot*. A Battle of Britain Hurricane ace, Wing Commander Ian Gleed DSO, DFC, also added his *Arise to Conquer* to the list. It was first published by Victor Gollancz Ltd. in May 1942.

All three books are excellent. Indeed, as Flight Lieutenant John Strachey says in his Foreword to Gleed's book, 'I cannot but suppose that both the contemporary reader and the future historian will turn to this book when they wish to know what the pilots who did this thing were like.' These books, then, provide a truly rich source of primary material for the modern reader. Sadly, what all three of these particular authors have in common is that none survived the war.

PREFACE

In this new edition of *Arise to Conquer*, I have endeavoured to describe more of Wing Commander Gleed's story, contextualising and fixing in time and space his comparatively short life and times, all built around a re-print of his original book. Importantly, my old friend, the late Squadron Leader Laurence Thorogood DFC, was a keen photographer and provided me copies of his snapshots, taken during those heady days when he flew Hurricanes alongside Ian Gleed. Many of these photographs appear in this book for the first time, providing us a window on the august past. They are as unique as Gleed's text.

Combined, we have a unique document which will, I am sure, enhance the understanding of those far-off days for those of us still fascinated by the Finest Hour's human experience.

Dilip Sarkar MBE, FRHistS

Prologue

The second child and first son of Dr Seymour Richard Gleed and his wife, Florence, was born at the family home, Brighton Lodge, Long Lane, Finchley, during the First World War on 3 July 1916. Joining an elder sister, Daphne, the new-born was called Ian Richard Gleed – who one day would become a decorated RAF fighter pilot.

Educated first at Tenterden Primary School, when aged twelve, young Ian attended Epsom College, where he boxed for the school, winning a trophy and the sobriquet 'Paper Weight' on account of his diminutive stature. Ian was not academic, but enjoyed sport, also playing tennis and rugby. He had an adventurous nature, joining the Public Schools' Exploring Society, with which, aged seventeen, he went on an expedition to Finnish Lapland in 1933, and Newfoundland the following year.

In 1934, Dr Gleed purchased a bungalow, a second home and family retreat, at High Cliff, Burlington Drive, Beltinge, at Herne Bay in Kent. There the intrepid Ian developed an interest in sailing, joining Herne Bay Sailing Club. He quickly becoming a competent yachtsman, so much so that his parents' twenty-first birthday present to him was a fourteen-foot sailing dinghy, *Spindrift*, in which he took first prize at the West Cliff Regatta's sailing dinghies' competition. In 1938, Ian would be fortunate enough to meet the great British author Somerset Maugham whilst holidaying in the South of France; Maugham loaned him a yacht in which to sail the Mediterranean. More importantly, it was Maugham who ignited an interest in writing, which four years later would manifest itself in Ian's *Arise to Conquer*.

The dark clouds of another world war were already gathering during the late 1930s – it was the period evocatively described by the historian Charles Loch Mowatt as the 'Devil's decade'. Whilst Ian Gleed's background might be considered privileged, his generation would soon be called upon to defend Britain's island shores.

Whereas his elder sister, Daphne, followed their father into medicine – no mean feat, either, for a female in what was a male dominated society and profession – at the age of fifteen Ian was inspired to become a pilot during a visit to the London Aeroplane Club at Hatfield aerodrome. Upon leaving Epsom, though, his academic achievements were insufficient to gain admission to RAF Cranwell, the service's college where professional career officers were trained.

There were, fortunately, other routes now available, owing to the 1936 Expansion Plan. War with Germany had looked increasingly likely from the mid-1930s onwards, and so various initiatives were launched to increase the junior service's establishment and reserve. Amongst these was the Short Service Commission (SSC), which, after retaking certain exams, and having started civilian flying training at Hatfield, Ian applied for. In the senior services, officers usually served for the duration of their working lives – hence the term 'Permanent Commission'. The SSC scheme, however, provided an opportunity for officers to serve a fixed contract of four years active service, followed by six on the reserve list. Such officers were only eligible to promotion so far as flight lieutenant but could transfer to a Permanent Commission upon successfully passing the required examination.

Ian Richard Gleed was notified of his acceptance for a SSC on 9 March 1936. He duly began flying training at the Civil Flying School, Filton. Having successfully completed this elementary course, on 4 May 1936, Ian was confirmed as an Acting Pilot

Officer (on probation), effective from 9 March 1936. A week later he reported to 8 Flying Training School at Montrose, for advanced flying training, by day and night. Pilot Officer Gleed was posted to 46 Squadron at Kenley on 25 December 1936. There he flew Gloster Gauntlet fighters; there could have been no better Christmas present.

The Gauntlet was the RAF's frontline fighter at that time. A biplane with an open cockpit, fixed pitch propeller and fixed undercarriage, armed with twin Vickers .303 machine-guns, with a top speed of 230 mph, this was a similar aircraft to those fighters of the First World War. On 9 October 1938, by which time Ian had flown the Gauntlet for nearly two years, and 46 Squadron was stationed at Digby, he was promoted to flying officer, and his SSC term extended to six years. In February 1939, 46 Squadron received a new monoplane fighter – a very different machine to the Gauntlet – and one with which Flying Officer Gleed was also to become intimately familiar.

Since 1931, following Supermarine designer RJ Mitchell's epic Schneider Trophy Air Race win with his S6.B monoplane, the Air Ministry had been keen to upgrade to a monoplane fighter, inviting designs for such a new aircraft. Hawker's designer, Sydney Camm, submitted a proposal for the 'Hawker Interceptor Monoplane', the requirement being for a short-range, defensive, fighter.

On 21 February 1935, the Air Ministry ordered a prototype of Camm's design, then updated the required specification for the new aircraft:

1. Had to be 40 mph faster than contemporary bombers at 15,000 feet.
2. Have eight forward-firing, wing-mounted, machine-guns, firing outside the propeller arc and 'by electrical means'.
3. Had to achieve a maximum speed of not less than 310 mph at 15,000 feet, at maximum power, with the highest speed possible between 5,000 and 15,000 feet.

4. Have the best possible climbing performance to 20,000 feet (although this was considered of secondary performance to 'speed and hitting power').
5. Be a steady gun platform.
6. Include the following 'special features': a) Enclosed cockpit; b) Cockpit heating; c) Night-flying equipment; d) Radio Telephony (R/T); e) Sufficient oxygen for a flight of two-and-a-half hours; f) Easily accessed and maintained machine-guns; g) Retractable undercarriage and tail-wheel; h) Wheel brakes.

Camm's creation completed a successful maiden flight from Brooklands on 6 November 1935. On 3 June the following year, the Air Ministry placed an order for 600 of Camm's design, the largest single such order ever placed in peacetime. In November 1937, 111 Squadron at Northolt became the first to be equipped with the new fighter: the Hawker 'Hurricane'.

When 46 Squadron received the Hurricane, Flying Officer Gleed and friends found that their new, modern, mount was nearly 100 mph faster than the Gauntlet, with improved visibility and manoeuvrability. Flight Lieutenant Peter Brothers, serving at Biggin Hill with 32 Squadron, remembered that the Hurricane was 'the first type I had ever flown with a retractable undercarriage and closed canopy, both great improvements. On my first flight I performed a few aerobatics and was impressed by the aircraft's immediate and smooth response. I knew straightaway that going to war in this machine was preferable to doing so in a biplane, which would have been suicidal.'

Peter was right. In Germany, the Me 109 single-seat monoplane fighter had been around since 1935; it had also seen combat during the Spanish Civil War. Events would soon prove that the Hurricane, and RJ Mitchell's Supermarine Spitfire, which was first taken on charge by 19 Squadron on 4 August 1938, arrived just in the nick of time.

By the time Britain and France declared war on Germany on 3 September 1939, following Hitler's invasion of Poland, Flying Officer Gleed and 46 Squadron had converted to their new Hurricanes and were well-familiar with the type. It is on that momentous day that 'Widge' Gleed – as Ian had become known on account of his fondness for the superlative 'wizard' and his short stature, this being a shortened version of 'Wizard Midget' – began his memoir, *Arise to Conquer.*

Foreword

It is a privilege to have the opportunity to contribute a foreword to this book by Wing Commander Gleed, under whom I had the honour to serve during the greater part of 1941. In these pages the reader will find, not so much described, as vividly reflected, the authentic atmosphere of the life of a fighter squadron of the Royal Air Force.

He will find one of the first accounts of the Battle of Britain set down by a pilot who took part in that extraordinary engagement. It is already clear that the Battle of Britain must ever remain one of the decisive engagements in world history. However long this second world war lasts, however gigantic, portentous and overwhelming its developments may be, the series of air engagements which took place over the eastern and southern parts of Britain between August and November 1940 must remain its first turning-point. They played, in much more desperate circumstances, the same role as was played by the Battle of the Marne in the first world war. The repulse of the air attack on Britain did not mean (by how many years, how many million deaths, how many prodigious events, we do not yet know) that the Fascist attempt to conquer the world had failed. On the contrary, the point at issue was that that attempt must have succeeded if the Battle of Britain had been lost. If the tiny number of British fighter squadrons which were at that time airworthy had then been overborne, none of the rest of the gathering of forces which will at last be adequate to the defeat of Nazi Germany and her Allies; neither the subsequent British recovery; nor the Russian resistance; nor the American entry into the war, could have taken place. The disproportion between the illimitable stake and the minute force involved is breath-taking.

I cannot but suppose that both the contemporary reader and the future historian will turn to this book when they wish to know what the pilots who did this thing were like. For it seems to me that once they have read it, they will know. They are here depicted with an artlessness which the most experienced authors will profoundly envy: 'Watty', eternally making his model aeroplanes in the dispersal huts (he is making them still, just about able, on the latest information, by unremitting toil to keep pace with his crashes); the resilient, the irrepressible 'Rubber' (he has just had to bale out again); Robbie, with his affectation of extreme disinterest in the war and his offhand charm (he is in a new job now); and the author himself, whom the reader will get to know best of all.

These, and just a few hundred more, were the pilots who did it. It was they who, when the telephone bells rang in the dispersal huts – when Ops. said, "One hundred plus; or a hundred and fifty plus; or two hundred plus, are crossing the coast" – jumped into their cockpits, took off and fought till the German aircraft turned back. In so doing, they settled the kind of lives which all of us, and our children, and probably their children, will lead.

We are bound to feel an insatiable curiosity as to what they were like, how they felt while they were doing it; and why they did it. Wing Commander Gleed, without for one moment trying to do so, answers these questions.

The simplest, and in my view the most exciting, thing which emerges is the fact that they felt frightened. That, if you come to think of it, is their ultimate claim to glory. If they had been Nazi or Japanese robots, mentally conditioned by some process of mass intoxication, some loathsome but effective scheme of mental mutilation, by which they had been dehumanised, hypnotised into actually liking death and destruction for the sake of some Führer, then the whole thing would have been incomparably less remarkable, and incomparably less worthwhile. But in fact, as the reader will see, they were, and are, just young Englishmen with the same likes, dislikes, hopes, fears and expectations as the rest of their generation. They were, and are, profoundly capable of the normal, constructive pursuits of peaceful existence; they are not one jot dehumanised or brutalised; they remain intensely individual, intensely themselves; and, nevertheless, they were able to do what they did. They are still doing it.

Flight Lieutenant John Strachey

Chapter 1

The Start

That morning the batman woke me with his usual smile. "Seven thirty, and a nice morning, sir." It was September 3rd, 1939. I was twenty-three. I turned on the wireless and listened to some music from Paris. After a few moments I heard Billy next door starting his French lessons on the gramophone, and at the end of the corridor 'Micky' was singing in the bath.

We all met at breakfast, some of us laughing and joking, others with hangovers, sullen and silent. Pat, the Flight Commander, was one of the latter. He told us to buck up, for we were all to be at readiness at eight-thirty, and had to taxi the machines from the hangars to dispersal positions.

'Micky', Pat and I drove the boys to the hangars. We clambered into our Hurricanes. There were shouts of "All clear!" and "Contact!" All the engines started except 'Dimmy' Simmonds': his prop was winding round with great streaks of flame pouring from the exhausts. We taxied slowly round the hangars, up the gentle grass slope, dodging the rough parts, lined the 'planes up along the hedge, switched off and wandered along to the recently put-up marquee.

"What were you doing last night, Pat? Out with a Popsie?" – "Yes, and I didn't get in till three, and I feel like death. Where the devil is Simmonds? Let's wander over and get the cars."

When we reached the hangar, we found that 'Dimmy's' 'plane was unserviceable with a dud magneto. More bad language from Pat. "How many does that leave us? Five in "B" Flight and six in "A"?"

I drove the car back to dispersal, tuning in the car radio. A Church service and a talk on gardens. "Damn! Wonder what time the news is."

It was a wizard morning, more like spring than autumn – blue sky, warm sun and a gentle breeze. The atmosphere in the Squadron was strangely cold; nobody talked very much. 'Dickie' (the Squadron Leader) is coming over. Wonder what he wants? "Good morning, sir. What's happening?" – "I don't know yet, except we're all at readiness; it looks like the real thing. Have you got a wireless out here? Chamberlain is broadcasting at eleven." – "I've got my car radio, sir." – "What's the time? I'll tune it in to Regional."

As Big Ben tolled out eleven, I felt a cold shiver run down my back. So, this was what we had trained for – war. The pilots crowded round, hedged in by the men; there was absolute silence as that somehow broken voice told us we were at war with Germany.

"Well, that's that, boys; you all know your jobs; I suppose we now say, 'Good hunting!' Stay at readiness until further orders. I'll try to get something fixed up about meals."

"Well, that's good-bye to my leave," Pat said. "I had got it all fixed to go to Skegness." The telephone rang in the marquee. Billy answered it. "No one is to leave the camp until further orders." – "Damn! That means good-bye to my date."

We lay out on the grass and thought. Our lunch came out in a Singer van: roast beef, but only lukewarm – curses from the boys. "Hell! I'm thirsty; let's send to the mess for some beer." – "You can't do that; we're only allowed soft drinks." – "Well, ginger beer would be better than nothing; bring half a dozen bottles; tell the steward to put them down to me."

"Anybody got anything to read? Bring some books – any old thing will do – and some writing-paper: might as well write home before it's blown to blazes."

The books and paper arrived; tea came out in the van. We still sat on the ground, waiting for a massed attack that we thought was sure to come.

THE START

Dusk came; we sat in the marquee, feeling none too warm or happy. "We must get some stoves," Pat said. I was annoyed, as I wanted to go to a "flick" in Lincoln.

The telephone rang: we were released till six thirty in the morning. "Hell's bells! What a hell of a time to get up!" When we got to the mess we were met with curses from the other Squadron. "Play me Squash, 'Micky'; we can have a swift game before dinner." I liked playing with 'Micky', because we were about dead equal, and always made each other run all over the place. I beat 'Micky' by one game. We ran to our rooms dripping with sweat. I yelled to the batman to grab me a bath, turned the wireless on – more news; what I heard of it was exactly the same as the four-o'clock version – stripped in front of the fire, shoved a dressing-gown on and sprinted along the corridor to the bath.

The mess was very crowded that night. Most people swallowed their dinner rather quickly, played a game of ping-pong or darts, and pushed off to bed. The night waiter was told to wake us at five forty-five – breakfast was at six.

I went to bed, tuned in to America and managed to hear a lot of atmospherics, a symphony orchestra, but no news. I turned the light out, after looking at the pictures of my racing dinghy, and wondered how long it would be before I sailed again. I loved sailing. With that thought I dropped off to sleep.

Digby, our Station, was on the flat plain that stretches for miles south-east of Lincoln. The horizon northwards was broken by a line of woods, and on clear days the spires of Lincoln Cathedral; around on all sides was flat agricultural land.

For days there had been no action. Our marquee had stoves, radio and a gramophone, which often played hot jazz, while the radio drawled out endless news bulletins and instructions about what to do in air-raids, blacking out car lights, etc. We were told that petrol rationing was very near.

"Hell!" said 'Micky'. "What shall I do with my confounded car? It does about twelve miles per gallon." Pat and I smiled; we both had

3

eight-h.p. jobs; 'Micky' had always been very fond of his big Buick. "I'm off on forty-eight hours' leave tomorrow; I'll store some in cans at home." We had wangled it that we got forty-eighters[1] every fortnight. We were all still convinced that our lives wouldn't last very long, so on our leaves we spent masses of cash and made the best of it.

The telephone rang; Pat answered. "What! How long for? O.K., we'll leave in about ten minutes." – "Where are we off to?" said 'Micky.' – "North Coates. We've got to do advanced readiness there; we'll come back here at dusk. Get your machines started." I grabbed a book and ran to my machine. "Start up." The fitter started for me. "Shall I put the book in the locker, sir?" (Later these lockers were covered by armour plating.) "Yes, please, and post this letter for me: God knows what North Coates is like."

Pat taxied his section out; I followed, signalling my two wing men to close formation. We took off in Flight formation, did one circuit of the 'drome and set off eastwards.

We soon saw the coast. To the left of us the wide mouth of the Humber shone in the sun; several ships were wending their way towards Hull. In front of us lay North Coates landing-field, seemingly right on the sandy shore. As we roared overhead, I could see that there was a sea-wall stretching right along the coast. We landed still in our close formation, turned around and taxied towards some wooden huts where we could see men waving. We swung round as we reached them, and faced into wind, ready for a quick take-off. There we stayed sitting in our cockpits listening to Pat binding[2] the ground station on the radio telephone. I squirmed round in my cockpit and produced my book from the locker. This looked as if it was going to be boring.

---

[1] Forty-eight hours' leave.

[2] To "bind" means to argue with, to try to get something out of, to admonish generally.

THE START

Pat started calling to us on the R.T.[3] "Hullo, Red and Blue aircraft! Prepare to start up with the self-starters; there is a convoy in our area which we may have to patrol. Keep R.T. watch. Is that understood, please? Over." Everyone answered in turn, "Your message received and understood. Over." The crackle of atmospherics and morse code did not help me to read my novel.

We didn't have to wait long. Suddenly above the crackles came, "Hullo, Jackal aircraft![4] Patrol convoy; now off Spurn Head. Over." Before the message was finished our engines had roared to life. Opening the throttles wide, we tore straight off down the 'drome. 'Wheels lifted; select wheels up; a gentle bang beneath my seat.' A red light on the dashboard told me my wheels were locked up. We headed out to sea.

It was hazy over the water: it wasn't until we were right over them that we saw the ships that we were meant to be protecting. As I stared down, I saw brilliant flashes from the escorting warships (a cruiser and two destroyers, I thought). "Hell! They're firing at us," came over the R.T. from Pat. "What about some evasive tactics?" I yelled back. Another clump of bursts went off just to the right of us. Damn them! This is getting beyond a joke.

We dived towards the sea and flew low just above the waves. There were black bursts just over our heads and columns of water going up either side of us. I thought it looked exactly like a naval battle on the films. We sheered off out to sea, climbed up to 5,000 feet again and patrolled up and down, keeping well out of gun-range from the ships. After an hour we received the orders on the R.T. to land. We dived back towards the land. As we circled the 'drome I noticed that our other Flight had arrived and were flying out towards the convoy. I wondered if they would get the same reception.

---

[3] R.T. stands for radio telephony. This is the method by which one pilot in his cockpit can talk to another. It can be used either in the air or when the machines are on the ground. Or the ground station can talk to the machines in the air, and they to it.

[4] Jackal is the code word meaning the aircraft of our particular squadron.

'Slow up, wheels down, a gentle bump as the wheels touch, a little brake.'

Then we taxied back to the wooden huts.

Our men had arrived, and had started refuelling the machines by the time we had undone our straps and jumped out. "Well, Pat, what do you think of that?"

"I was wearing my finger out, flashing the letter of the day on the morse key, but they didn't seem to take any damned notice," said 'Mickey'. "So was I," everyone asserted. Then the Flight Sergeant came up and said there was a lump of shrapnel in Sergeant Lawson's machine; that shook us all a bit.

We went into the wooden huts, which had coal stoves in them, and warmed ourselves up. "Try that 'phone and see if we can produce any lunch from the mess." – "O.K., Pat." 'Dimmy' got on to the mess, and they sent up some rather cold stew; it didn't look particularly appetising, but we ate it with relish.

Just as we finished lunch the other Flight landed from their patrol, and we had to return to our cockpits and be ready to take off at a second notice on the R.T. They came and chatted to us when they had had their lunch. Billy told me that they also had been shot at, so had carried out their patrol well out to sea.

So, the day went and dusk fell. With dusk came the orders, "Return to base and land there." We flew back as a squadron, four sections in vic. I was leading the last section, and thought how glorious the sky looked above the setting sun, and how peaceful the world seemed as seen from the sky.

We were happier in the mess that night; we felt that we had done a job, and that perhaps after all we would see something of the war.

A week passed before the Squadron met action; it was in the afternoon. We had just been relieved by "A" Flight when we heard the ground station say that twelve enemy aircraft were about 20 miles east of the convoy that we had been patrolling. Dickie, the Squadron

Leader, was leading the other flight, and I heard his voice say, "Message received and understood," then silence.

We landed as quickly as possible, taxied to the bowsers and shouted to the crews to beat all records refuelling. We stayed in the cockpits and listened to the R.T. The ground station came through again and told Jackal Leader that the "bandits" were very close.

After a few minutes faintly came, "Tally-ho! Twelve enemy float 'planes sighted to the south of us; am going in to attack," then "Jackal aircraft line astern for attack, echelon starboard go." Then silence.

Pat started his engine; all the 'planes were refuelled. All our engines roared to life, and the 'planes leapt into the air, making a bee-line out to sea. Very faintly I heard Dickie talking on the R.T. – something about someone down in flames. Theirs or ours? I wondered. Then another message, "They have gone out to sea; all aircraft return to base." I thought 'That means that they are split up. God! I hope they are all O.K.'

We turned back to land. What a damned pity that we hadn't been with "B" Flight! 'Wonder what they've got. God, I hope everyone is O.K.!' We had taxied in and were clambering out when "B" Flight's first 'planes came in. "A" and "B". That's Dickie (our Squadron Leader) and Billie. We crowded round their 'planes as they switched their engines off.

"What happened, sir?" Pat asked.

"Twelve Heinkel 115s, big torpedo-carrying float-'planes. I saw them coming round into the sun, and went into line astern. Then into echelon for number three attack. They never saw us coming. The one I attacked caught fire and crashed. I chased another one which was trying to run for it. I saw him drop his torpedo, then I caught him. Two of the crew baled out. Then the 'plane went straight in. I steep-turned, and saw the two floats bob up, and a large patch of oil. I'm damned if I could see where the blokes who baled out landed. Well, Billie, that was easy, wasn't it?"

"It was just perfect, sir; if only we'd had the whole Squadron, none of them would have got away. I gave mine a long burst; he fired back and hit my wing, then dived straight in."

We all stared at Billie's right wing; it had two bullet-holes in it. One had made quite a large hole coming out of the top of the wing.

"Here come the others. Four. Good show! That's everyone."

They all taxied in and jumped out.

"That was wizard," 'Micky' cried as he ran up to us. "I got a flamer. I gave him one long burst and up he went; he slowed down so quickly that I nearly hit him. That was a grand attack that you did, sir."

The others ran up from their 'planes. They had all knocked one down and were very excited. It seemed to have been very easy, the only opposition coming from one gun fired from the rear cockpit. The rear gunners must have been quite good shots, for they had hit the engine panels of two of our 'planes; luckily both where the armour plating was, so no damage was done.

Pat, the "B" Flight boys, and I were very sick that we hadn't been in the fight. It sounded so very easy to shoot the hulking great float-'planes. Still, the Squadron had been in action and done its stuff. Seven 'planes destroyed for no losses seemed too good to be true. 'God, I hope that they send some more tomorrow when we are on patrol!' We got back into our cockpits very keyed up, waiting for action. It didn't come.

That evening we flew back in even tighter formation than usual and dived low over the aerodrome. All the ground staff were as pleased as Punch; our "B" Flight men ragged us and asked when we were going to see something; we cursed at them in return, and laughed at the other Flight, who were trying to make out combat reports. That night there was a terrific party in the mess.

One night, after several weeks of uneventful convoy patrols, Dickie 'phoned me and asked me over to his house for some drinks after dinner. I thought it a bit unusual, as Dickie generally had a crowd of us there when he "threw out a boat".

I walked to his house, which was about a quarter of a mile from the mess. It was a pitch-black night, although the stars seemed very bright. I rang the bell. The maid answered the door and told me that I was expected.

"Good evening, Leeds. I have got some news for you," Dickie said as I stepped into the room. "You have been posted as Flight Commander to a new Squadron forming at Sutton Bridge. Congratulations!" – "Hell! That's grand, sir, but I'll be sorry to leave all the boys." He smiled. "So shall I; I'm posted there, too, as Station Commander." – "Well, sir, congratulations! That's wizard." – "Have a beer, Leeds, and we'll drink to our new jobs." – "Cheers, sir!" – "Cheerio!"

Dickie told me that he had to be there the following day, and that I had to be there the day after.

Sutton Bridge wasn't very far away; it used to be an armament training camp, and we had been there as a Squadron a year before for a fortnight's shooting practice.

Chapter 2

A Fall

The next day I started packing. I had been at Digby for just on two years, and had accumulated a terrific pile of odds and ends. Thomas, my batman, did most of the work. I should miss him: he had been with me for over a year, and had grown to know all the little things I liked. I thought of Pat, 'Micky' and Billie. We had been together in the Squadron for over three years now; it would be like going to school again.

Bangs at the door. "Come on, 'Widge',[5] we've got barrels of beer for you; we've got a bottle of pop for Dickie; we knew you would prefer beer." The boys had got a farewell party fixed for us in the mess; it was 'Micky's' cheery voice.

We had a good dinner, with lots to drink – sherry, champagne and port; then, after that, beer. As the night wore on the party got more riotous. I felt strangely sad and lonely. We had trained together, and we wanted to fight together so much. Tomorrow I should be seeing new faces, new pilots whom I would have to teach to fight. The party ended at one. We carried Dickie to bed; I could still just walk. I tore my clothes off and dropped into bed and straight off to sleep. Needless to say, I woke with a hell of a head.

I left at ten the next morning, after having said good-bye to all the boys, the N.C.O.s and the men. I was sad. I patted the tail of my Hurricane, which I had had since we had been re-equipped with them a year before. We had had many happy hours together: in the good old

---

[5] This is my nickname; I don't know why.

days of peace, I had used her for flying down to Manston for week-ends of racing my fourteen-footer dinghy. "Well, good-bye, Digby. I'll come and visit you."

The car was piled high with luggage. As I drove out of the camp, I wondered what I had left behind in the way of personal belongings, apart from my friends. Although it was the middle of November, it was warm and sunny. I stopped when I got to Sleaford to buy a new wireless aerial – I was very fond of my wireless. Then on along the long, straight, flat roads of the Fens. The car was going well. I looked at the new stripes sewn on my cuff by Thomas. Flight Lieutenant at last.

There followed a tedious wait before the new Squadron got its fighter aircraft. Then one day Dickie met me with a great smile all over his face. "Hullo, 'Widget'. You're getting Spitfires – six are waiting for collection now." – "Damn good show, sir." I should have preferred to have Hurricanes, as I knew them, and I had never flown a Spitfire; I should soon learn.

The C.O., I, and some other pilots were to collect the first three the following day. As soon as we had landed, we taxied over to the hangar, where three spotless new Spitfires were parked outside, all ready for us to take off – except, of course, for the rather boring business of checking the inventories.

We got that over as quickly as possible, started the engines, ran them up to full revs to see that the magnetos were doing their stuff, taxied out and off in rather wide formation. James, the other Flight Commander, was close into the C.O., but I wanted to feel what they were like on the controls before I closed formation.

The take-off felt impressive, as I opened the throttle and felt a kick in the back caused by the terrific acceleration. Roaring along the ground for a very short distance with one wing down caused by the torque of the airscrew, we came unstuck. Moving the selector level to wheels-up position, I pumped the handle which operated the hydraulic system; as I pumped, I found the whole 'plane going up and down. Hell! she is sensitive on the controls.

Soon I had settled down to things at cruising speed. I found that the controls were similar to a Hurricane, so I felt quite at home. Quick glances at the instruments told me that we were going about thirty miles an hour faster than the Hurricane would have been doing at the same throttle-opening: we were certainly getting a move on. In what seemed an incredibly short time Sutton Bridge hove in sight. We closed into very tight formation. I caught a rapid glimpse of the hangars as they flashed by.

The C.O. gave the break-up signal; he went down to land, while James and I stayed up and did a few aerobatics. Then into land I went; with a bit of a bump and a gentle application of the brakes I made the grade all right. It felt like flying an American racing machine, or, at least, how I imagined it felt like flying a racing machine – very different from the much bigger Hurricane. All I wanted now was a Jerry machine to shoot at. But it was going to be some time before I saw my first Hun.

One afternoon when the snow was still on the ground, I wandered into the mess to get the post. I met the Doc, and told him that so far, we had got everyone off on their first solo flights in Spitfires without an accident; there were only two more left, and we were sending them up that afternoon. I touched wood so that our luck would still hold.

Shortly after, the two "Spitters" were roaring off a few practice turns; then into land they came – both perfect landings, as first solo flights on new types often are. I climbed into one of the new ones that had only been flown for short test flights near the ground. One of my jobs was to test them at rated altitude, about 18,000 feet.

This afternoon it was cold, with a biting wind and rather a lot of fairly thick cloud at about 5,000 – good enough for a test. I climbed quickly up, going flat out. The aerodrome gradually grew smaller. The visibility was good: I could see the whole of the Wash. The tide was out, and the sandbanks were dry. What a place to sail! I should be permanently on a sandbank there! Soon

A FALL

I was in a layer of cloud, then, after about 1,000 feet, I shot out of the whiteness into warm sunshine. There was another layer of very high cloud, with large holes of brilliant blue sky. I climbed in large circles. The clouds beneath me looked very beautiful in the sun. Up and up; temperature O.K., everything O.K. As soon as I reached 18,000 feet I levelled out and checked all instruments. All looked well. I opened up gently until I was at full throttle. Boosts O.K., Revs. 2850, speed just right.

One fault: she seems to be flying a bit right wing low. Can fix that as soon as I land, Brrrrr! It's a bit cold up here; let's go down. Throttle back a bit, stick forward.

I nosed down into a gentle dive; the speed rose. I adjusted the compass to steer a northerly course, then started a gentle left-hand turn.

'Close radiator, down we go. Crack! Christ! What's that?'

I was slung forward in the cockpit, my safety-straps just stopping me hitting the dashboard. I tried to lift my head, but couldn't. Bang! Blackness.

'Why can't I sleep? Wonder what the time is? Where am I?'

Everything was black – very black.

'Where am I? When did I land? And what have I been doing? Christ, I must be in the air! Where's the rip-cord?'

It was very strange: there was no dropping sensation. It was absolutely dark, and I couldn't feel any rushing air.

'Now feel carefully for the rip-cord. Keep cool. Remember the bloke who was found with his side ripped out and the parachute not opened. Oh, God, where is the rip-cord? Steady.'

At last, I felt the metal square. It felt queerly warm. I tugged hard. Felt a jerk. Then nothing.

'Let me wake up; this is a hellish dream. Bump, bump. Oh, hell, I must have fallen out of bed! No. Let me think. Bump. This is hell. Wake up, you fool! You've baled out and are being pulled along the ground by your parachute. Bang the quick release.'

I slapped the quick-release box, felt the harness slip from my body. Thank God I was now still. I clung to the grass, while the world seemed to heave and sway beneath me.

'I'm blind – stone blind. My left arm hurts like hell, and my right leg.'

My right shoe had fallen off somewhere. There was snow on the ground; my sock got wet.

'I can't stand this pain; I shall be sick. Christ, let me think. Left arm seems broken, right leg broken, and I'm stone blind. Unless somebody comes soon, I shall freeze to death. I'd better start crawling. Oh, God, please let me see soon. It's so dark.'

I did start crawling, dragging myself along the ground with my right arm, keeping my left arm still against my side.

'Oh, it's cold! the wind seems as if it were cutting me in pieces. My helmet's still on; perhaps it's over my eyes.'

I tore it off; my hair was sticky. Blood, I supposed.

'Oh, God, I'm still blind. Please let me see. Why doesn't somebody come?'

I crawled. The earth settled down. I no longer felt that I had to hang on to the grass to stop myself flying into the air.

'Thank God, here comes somebody.'

I heard voices in the distance: "Gawd, doesn't 'e look a bluedy mess?"

"I may look a bloody mess; I feel bloody awful. Is a doctor coming?" I shouted. – "Doctor's coming soon."

"Is anyone else in the 'plane, chum?" – "No, I'm alone," I groaned back.

"Cover me up with something, I'm freezing. Where's the 'plane?"

"It be orl in pieces," another voice chipped in.

"That's better; thanks." A heavy blanket or coat was tenderly placed on me. "Oh God, my leg! – That's better"; they adjusted the coats. God, it was cold!

"'Ere comes the boss." The sound of a car broke through the pain.

"Get me to a doctor, please get me to a doctor," I moaned.

This can't go on for long; I shall die.

The car drew near and stopped. A door slammed. "Is he alright?" another voice enquired. "Yes, I'm O.K. Is there a doctor coming?"

"He'll be here in a minute, old chap."

I lay and thought. I was in a mess, then gradually the pitchy darkness lightened. 'Thank God, my sight is coming back.'

A grey screen seemed to flash across my eyes; gradually the grey turned to white. A few flakes of snow were falling on my face. I lifted my head and saw the three men, with an Austin Ten in the background. Thank God I could see. What a marvellous thing sight is! I saw now that I was covered with some sacking and a coat.

"Lift me up and put me in the car; I'm freezing here."

"All right, old chap."

They lifted me carefully; I found my arm didn't hurt too much if I kept it absolutely still; my leg was hellish, and my head felt as if it was falling off.

There was a hurried conference going on outside. They decided to drive me to the farm. The bumps as we drove very slowly over the field nearly knocked me out. Soon we stopped by a house. A kindly woman brought me some coffee. I drank it slowly, and felt better.

Once more I heard a car engine; this time it was an ambulance and a R.A.F. doctor from the hospital. Very tenderly they put me on a stretcher and pushed me in the back. A jab in the arm told me that at last they had given me morphia. Through a haze I noticed that when we stopped, I was carried head first through big doors, then laid on a table.

I told them who I was, asked them to ring Sutton Bridge and send telegrams to Pam and my mother, saying that I was only slightly hurt. Then everything faded.

I woke up in a bed, feeling incredibly hot and weak, lying flat on my back, my left arm in plaster, right leg and head swathed in bandages. A nurse was sitting by the bed; she leant over me and said, "You're all right, Laddie."

Chapter 3

Good-Bye

After three weeks in hospital, I was worrying the M.O. to let me have a "Board" and get back to work. He was rather loath to do this until he was dead certain that I should pass. Eventually, after a month, the great day came. Every day of the previous week I had been holding my breath for practice, one of the tests being to hold your breath for a minute – much easier said than done.

At the Board things seemed to go well. I passed all the tests with what I thought were flying colours. When I had clothed myself, I was told to go outside and wait for the result. I didn't like the look of that at all. Outside I went, pacing up and down, waiting for what seemed hours, before the door was opened and in I went again. Thereupon I received a long lecture on teetotalism, and was finally told that I had not passed the exam completely, and would have to have another one after a further three weeks. I would be allowed to fly, dual only, and therefore would be allowed to return to my unit.

I left the room cursing hard under my breath. What the Devil was the use of returning to my unit – a single-seater fighter Squadron – if I was only allowed to fly dual? Well, after a farewell party over the week-end, I left Torquay for Uxbridge, where I had to report for further orders, and where, with luck, I should be granted some leave.

Uxbridge did not fail me. I drove into the camp at ten-thirty, having stayed the previous night at home, and drove out again with a ten-days' leave pass, at exactly eleven-thirty. I was very pleased. Off to Kent I went to stay a week-end with the girl friend.

GOOD-BYE

It was grand being with Pam again. We went to all the old spots together – to Herne Bay, where my boat, *Spindrift*, was laid up. With the help of several old boatmen friends, we had her outside the Sailing Club, rigged ready for launching. We went for our first sail on a rough, blustery day, and loved it.

Officially, sailing was only permitted in a small area. This did not suit us at all, as we wanted to sail round the foreland to Broadstairs, so that Pam could sail her there throughout the summer. We made many enquiries as to what chances there were of getting permission, and found that the chances were small. So, we decided that we would give ourselves permission, and sail her round the first fine day.

The second day after our decision broke fine, with a grand sailing breeze. We hurtled off to Herne Bay in the car, taking a friend with us to bring the car back. Launched *Spindrift*, made sure that plenty of food and drink was on board, upped sail, and off we went. It was a wizard day – warm sunshine and a full sailing breeze. We wondered how far we would get, and how many mines we would hit en route. Soon we were past Reculver Towers, where we were stared at by the coastguards. We tried to look as nonchalant as possible. On past the long, low-lying coastline of the marshes.

Soon Herne Bay pier was disappearing beneath the skyline and Margate pier growing close. We were worried about Margate, as we knew that several patrol-boats were kept there. The last thing we wanted was to be intercepted and dragged into that not-too-pleasant harbour. Past the pier we sailed and no boat appeared; all was well. The next stop was Broadstairs harbour.

The wind blew harder as we rounded the foreland; by sitting out with the aid of our toe-straps we just managed to still carry full sail. Little Broadstairs harbour hove in sight; we sailed in just in time for tea. The car was there to meet us, so, after carrying the gear to the Sailing Club, we drove off to the house for tea. How grand it was to sail, to drive one's own car, and eat a large tea sitting over the fire, dreaming happy dreams of the future.

The time seemed to fly like a flash of lightning: it seemed only yesterday that I had arrived; but today was the end of my leave. Tomorrow I should return to my old unit, to fly dual only. Hell! for how long? Who knows? Pam and I were together the last night at my home in London. We went to the "flicks" and had a good laugh at Walt Disney's latest masterpiece.

The morning came with swift farewells, on to the road to ——, where my old Squadron was now stationed. I had never been there. I wondered what life would have in store for me now. I felt as fit as a fiddle, and longed to fly again.

When I arrived all the boys and the C.O. were very pleased to see me. Things were going well for them, but not for me. "A" Flight was now commanded by another Flight Lieutenant, whom I didn't know. The C.O. told me that he was very sorry but couldn't do anything about it. I understood. Anyway, I wasn't even fit for flying yet, according to the doctors.

By this time the big German advances had begun, Holland and Belgium had been invaded. There was still very little activity over England: a few 'planes had been shot down on raids on the Firth of Forth. One night a German mine-laying 'plane crashed at Clacton, killing several people, and knocking down a row of houses.

Suddenly the war was brought to our doorstep: a Hurricane Squadron at the 'drome was ordered to go on an offensive patrol to the Hook of Holland. Within the hour of receiving the orders they were off, flying eastwards in close Squadron formation.

It seemed ages before they returned. They came back one by one. We counted them as they roared over the 'drome – five, six, seven; then nothing. The afternoon turned into evening; the sun set with a livid glow. Five never returned. They had run into a terrific number of Messerschmitts. The pilots that I talked to seemed shaken; they said that they had never seen so many 'planes in the air at the same time. One moment they were flying alone with nothing else in the sky; the next moment the sky was full of 'planes with black crosses on, spitting death from machine-guns and cannons. They told me that they could hear the cannons firing at them. They had seen nine Jerries go down definitely, and thought that many more had failed to get home. Soon they had finished their ammunition. Turning for home, they had been chased half-way across. Five of them had fallen into the sea; the last one to go had been shot down in flames only about thirty miles from the coast. Their Squadron Leader and one of their Flight Commanders were amongst those who never came back.

After that episode I somehow felt guilty that I wasn't fit. I kept on badgering the C.O. to speed up my Board.

A few days later I wandered into the office to see if there was anything in, or any work to do. Nothing of interest. So, I was idly amending K.Rs. and A.C.I.s, sticking slips of paper in with a huge glue-pot and brush, and bored stiff. By this time even the kind C.O. was getting a bit browned off[6] with me hanging around doing nothing.

In came an orderly with a postagram slip. The C.O. looked at it and read it out aloud: "Flight Lieutenant Leeds posted to 87 Squadron, B.E.F., France. To proceed to Halton on receipt of signal for medical board. Report to Uxbridge following day if fit for full flying duties. Authority Air Ministry."

To say the least of it, there was a flap: it was now just past ten, nothing was packed, and of course I had no petrol coupons. I dashed out to my car, hurtled off to the mess, told my batman to get all his colleagues to help and pack everything, ready to move off in an hour's time. Then rushed off to the mess to fix up my mess bill and clearance certificates; then off to Headquarters. More signatures on the clearance certificates, petrol coupons from the Station adjutant, out like a flash, down the road to the Squadron Office, a few very quick words of thanks, and Good-bye.

"Say good-bye to the boys, please, sir. I hope you have all the luck in the world and good hunting. Thanks again for everything."

---

[6] "Browned off" means fed up.

Back to the mess. Everything was packed. Good show! Shove it all in the car. Poor little car sagged a bit at the back; she still would go like a bomb. Then out past the sentries on the open road heading across country for Halton, driving like hell and trying to read an A.A. book at the same time; collecting my rather scattered thoughts. Christ, what a hurry! My hands were filthy, as I had filled the car with oil and water as petrol was pumped in at the first garage.

Somehow, I was going to pass that medical, even if I had to drug the doctor to sign the certificate; then I would drive home, stay the night there and go to Uxbridge the following morning. So far, I hadn't even warned home. The C.O. told me that as soon as I had passed the Board, I was to ring him and he would get on to the Air House and let them know that things were O.K.

Poor Pam! she would be hellishly upset. She was very brave, and as we loved each other so much, she would be glad for me. 'Damn the car! Why won't it go faster? Blast these A.A. maps; they are bloody awful. Why the hell must everyone I ask the way from be a stranger in these parts?' At last, very exhausted, at about one fifteen I drove into the camp at Halton.

Halton is one of those terrifically big camps, with squads of men marching all over the place. I always found it very difficult to find the way about on camps like that; you couldn't very well ask one of the squads the way, and sometimes it was ages before you came upon a single airman! Eventually I found a sentry, who directed me to the mess. I definitely wanted a wash, and thought that I had better have some lunch, although I didn't feel much like anything.

The mess there used to be one of the Rothschild mansions – a very spacious place, surrounded by lovely grounds. After washing, I wandered into the dining-room for a quick lunch. Being late, there was hardly anyone else there, so I lunched alone.

After a hurried lunch I asked one of the waiters to direct me to the board room; actually, it consisted of many rooms filling a wooden building. I went into the main door, where I signed my name and a clerk rushed off to see if I was on their list to be examined that afternoon. To my intense relief, I was. I was then shown into a waiting-room where five or six other officers were sitting reading magazines.

R.A.F. medical exams are noted for their long duration: for hours you are kept waiting; each specialist sees you at, if you are lucky, an hour's interval; sometimes the whole Board takes a couple of days. Most of the chaps there had been there the whole morning, and all seemed only about half-way through their tests. I sat down and waited.

The orderly appeared periodically and escorted one or other of the officers to different rooms, some to blow up the mercury – one of the tests that I most feared. Nothing happened to me. I chatted to some of the others. Three of them were there as they were browned off with being at readiness, and had taken rather too strongly to drink. They seemed to be under the impression that if they failed, they would be slung out, and have to join the army as privates. I wondered what blacks they had put up; they must have been pretty bad to be in their present position.

At last, my turn came. I went into a room, where I stripped, and was pummelled all over the place. I noticed that my feet weren't exactly clean. Why the hell hadn't I had a bath that morning? I would have done if I had known that I was going to have a Board that day; anyway, it was too late now – let's hope the doc. wouldn't notice too much. I dressed again, then back to the waiting-room. At this rate I should never get finished today.

Actually, I didn't have long to wait: the orderly came in again and told me that I was to go first for all the further tests. I hated the colour tests. You have to look at pages in a small book which are covered with strange coloured dots; on each page is a letter or figure which you have to read; some of them are hellishly difficult to see. That seemed O.K., so back to the waiting-room. Another short wait, then to my most-dreaded test: blowing mercury up to a certain height in a tube and holding it there as long as possible. My usual alibi for failing to do this on my annual medicals was that I had small lungs. I didn't think that that would go down so well this time. After nearly bursting my guts I held it up for a minute; then, just to finish me off, I had to hold my breath for another minute; this I just managed to do. I felt as if I was going to burst. I asked the doc. if I was O.K. He said "Yes." 'Well,' I thought, sweating like a pig as I put my shirt on, 'so far, so good.'

Another half-hour in the waiting-room before it was my turn to see the President of the Board. Whilst I waited, a couple of the browned-off types interviewed him, and came out after being told that they had failed and would be permanently off flying. I began to feel gloomy. They talked about having to join the army as privates. I felt slightly sick, with a very heavy feeling in my tummy. I prayed very hard that when my turn came, I should be told that I was A.1 for full flying duties. At last, the orderly called my name, and in I went.

The old boy looked rather nice. I noticed that he had all my documents on the desk before him. "You have passed your Medical, and you are fit for full flying duties." I can't tell you how much those words meant to me. After a word of advice, I was handed the slip of paper which would prove to anyone who asked that I was absolutely serviceable. I went out to the hall and asked the orderly where was the nearest telephone that I could use. He said in one of the doctors' offices, and showed me where.

It was only a matter of minutes before I was through to the Old Man at Martlesham. He was still in his office waiting for the call from me. It seemed to me that he was nearly as pleased as I was. He told me that he would fix everything, and that all I should have to do was to report to Uxbridge by ten the following morning.

I was really happy for the first time since my crash, as I ran to my car, leapt in and started off down the road for home. The country looked very clean and beautiful in the late winter sunlight. "Oh, to be in England now that Spring was here." Who the devil had said that? I was damned if I knew; anyway, I should be in La Belle France. I wondered, as I drove, if there would be any chance to get any leave to visit my friends in the South of France. I thought a couple of weeks there, after a month of flying to get the touch back, would do me a lot of good; anyway, I ought to be able to wangle a few hot parties in Paris; I hoped that I wouldn't be too far away from that gay city.

Soon I was driving up the old familiar main road to my house. I wondered how my mother would take it. In the Great War she had seen my father off to France. Now it was my turn. The world did not seem to have progressed much. One thing that I thanked God for was that this wasn't a war to end wars or to make a land fit for heroes to live in: this was a bitter war; we were fighting for our lives. I wanted to fight.

The family were waiting on the doorstep at my home when I arrived. My mother, father and sister all seemed very cheery. They immediately started helping me pack. My mother, of course, suggested taking all sorts of underclothes and things; my father kept on saying what he had taken, so managed to stop the terrific pile of equipment that my mother had amassed. Daphne, my sister, 'phoned up Pam for me and asked her to come and stay the night with us – rather a tall order for her, as she was at her home at Broadstairs. She said that she would be arriving at Victoria at ten that evening, and would I meet her? Of course, I would.

After having a terrific struggle with my camp kit – a model anything but official; as my official model had disappeared some years before, I had bought a rather highly coloured garden settee. I thought that it would cheer the place up wherever I was. Unfortunately, it did not fold into a small palliasse, which my father very kindly produced – a relic of the last war. Anyway, after hours of struggling, all was packed and everyone was satisfied with the contents, two rolls of lavatory paper included. Actually, the amount of luggage looked as if I was setting off for a cruise round the world; still, perhaps all would be well. Heaven alone knew what would happen if I had to fly across. I should have to leave it all behind. Anyway, why worry? It would be a good excuse for going to Paris for a shopping – ahem – expedition.

I rushed up to the station to meet Pam. Her train was punctual, so we were soon back home again. My parents, after a lot of talking, pushed off to bed and left us to ourselves. That night we sat up until the early hours. We had so much to talk about before we pushed off to bed.

All too soon came breakfast time. Somehow everyone seemed rather too cheerful. We all loaded my car up, as I had arranged to drive to Uxbridge in my own car, and for my father to collect it from there as soon as he possibly could. Soon came the time to say goodbye, my mother just managing to keep the tears back; Daphne blew her nose rather a lot, and Pam and Dad smiled. They wanted to come to the station, to finally see me off, but I thought otherwise. I had arranged with Pam that we should have a few seconds together somehow before I left for France.

I drove like hell to Uxbridge along the very straight road past Northolt aerodrome, and was soon at the entrance to the big R.A.F. depot. I was a very much happier and prouder person than I had been the month before when I had been here to get my leave. To my surprise, I soon discovered that there was only one other chap going across with me; we were to be in charge of three hundred men, and were to sail from port X to port Z on the other side that evening.

It was an extremely warm spring day – at least, we thought so, because we had to chase here, there and everywhere, getting revolvers, kit-bags, first-aid kits and field pay-books. Whichever office we went to we found that we had to go to another one right the other side of the camp. In the intervals I wondered if I should ever see Pam again. We had been nearly engaged for over a year now; in the good old days of peace, we had sailed together, and had dreamed happy dreams of the future. I loved her now more than ever; but life and death seemed very close together these days; my forty-eighters seemed to go like a flash; the life of a fighter pilot in the last war was meant to be a fortnight. I wondered what it would be this time when the blitz came – not much longer.

GOOD-BYE

One thing was certain in my mind: we mustn't be married. Happiness, real happiness of peace days, was past. In the swift leave we had tried to regain the feeling of the old days; we had laughed a lot. All the time the shadow of war was there. I wished with all my heart and soul that Pam was there smiling at me. I must do my job first – help win the war – then start off a new life with a happy marriage, if I was still alive.

Chapter 4

Combats Before Lunch

As the French express roared across the countryside, I thought what a strange world it was: a little while ago I had been in a damned uncomfortable troop-train; now I was in a very comfortable train, eating a delicious roast chicken and sipping champagne. Soon it was dark. I was surprised how slack the French were about black-out – nearly every village had many windows showing bright lights; the train itself was only blacked out with blinds which half the time were up, as passengers peered out.

After several halts, the train drew into the outskirts of Lille, and steamed very slowly into the station. As soon as I was on the platform I heard the crack of anti-aircraft, and the dull thud of bombs bursting in the distance; through the glass roof of the station, I could see searchlights sweeping the sky. I thought, 'Well, this is a good welcome to the war.' I wandered along to the R.T.O.'s office and tried to get the aerodrome on the 'phone.

After about half an hour I got through to the 87 Squadron mess. The Adjutant said that the best thing to do was to stay the night in Lille and report in the morning; he suggested that I should stay at the Metropole, and he would send transport at ten in the morning.

The French didn't seem to take much notice of the air-raid, except that this time the black-out was a hundred per cent effective, for the simple reason that all the lights were turned off. The station was absolutely crammed with refugees; it was with the utmost difficulty that I managed to get out of the station, after parking my main luggage with the R.T.O.

I soon found the Metropole – a tall, rather smart hotel with a lot of glass and chromium plate in the foyer. The receptionist seemed to think that it was a hell of a joke when I asked for a room – there wasn't a room in the place. She told me that I would find some R.A.F. officers in the bar. She was right. The so-called bar was a low room with crowds of tables, overflowing with uniforms and French girls.

A table of slightly tight R.A.F. blokes hailed me and stood me a drink. "You're the new Flight-Lieutenant for 87, are you? Well, ol' boy, you stick along with us; we're staying somewhere in this goddamned town tonight, and will take you out to the 'drome in the morning."

"Damn it, ol' boy, I'm off after that one" – so off went one of the blokes after a very ropy blonde. A few drinks and I was feeling muzzily pleased with life; all I wanted now was a damned nice bed. The party was gradually growing smaller, as one by one the boys disappeared with various women. I gathered that most of the blokes were from 504 Squadron, who that afternoon had shot down about fourteen Jerries, but had lost six of themselves, including the C.O.

Eventually there were only two of us left. The other bloke felt like me, so we pushed off in search of a pub that wasn't full. We found that we couldn't walk more than a few feet before we were accosted by women – the place was swarming with prostitutes. Neither of us was feeling at all inclined that way that night. At last, we found quite a decent small hotel which gave us a double room and bath for fifty francs, cash before you sleep. As it was now in the early hours of the morning, this place seemed empty of the crowd of women.

The sun was streaming through the window when I woke. Petit dejeuner was brought up to our room. We ate it hurriedly, and went downstairs, where we found an R.A.F. driver with a Citroen van. We bumped through Lille, then down a small road leading to the country. My companion left us at the first small village. We bumped on across the cobbles for about another half-mile, then turned into a drive lined with trees, round a bend, and stopped by what looked to me to be a cricket pavilion. Several types were lying about in deck chairs.

A tough-looking pilot was adjusting a small petrol engine of a model 'plane. I soon discovered that he was 'Watty', one of "A" Flight boys – "A" Flight was to be my flight. I introduced myself rather nervously. They seemed pleased to see me. After many questions of what London looked like, I managed to hear something about my new Squadron.

No.87 Squadron had come out to France right at the beginning of the war, in company with 85; they had been together at Debden for several years before the war. They were a happy bunch, and loved France. Terrific parties were had in Paris. The Squadron had moved around to various 'dromes – Le Touquet, Senan, Lille, Seclen, Amiens. All these 'dromes became familiar to the pilot boys. Each place had its amusing memories: Le Touquet, where the inevitable "Cock" overshot and fell into a reservoir; Senan, where 'Robbie" landed with his wheels up – "Just forgot them, old boy." France liked them and they liked France. Life was rosy and spring was coming.

They had lots of adventures but little action. Flight-Lieutenant David Rhodes, "B" Flight's Commander, shot down a Heinkel – the first one to be shot down in France – and received the Croix de Guerre avec Palme and the D.F.C.

The C.O., 'Dusty' Miller and Beaver force-landed in Belgium five miles the wrong side of the frontier on the sands at La Panne. They were jumped upon by the Belgian army and whipped away to a castle in Brussels. They were soon called the mad English boys, because every afternoon they went for a run round the grounds. It was a mediaeval place, surrounded by a moat. Every day they made their run a bit later; gradually they worked it that they didn't get back until after dark. The British Consul and various friends visited them and made secret arrangements. One evening they ran very hard, slipped down the bank of the moat, swam it, ran like hares, hid in a wood for a couple of hours, then picked up the car driven by their Belgian friend, who hid them where they could slip across the French frontier undetected. Back to the Squadron they came, dressed in the most fantastic clothes.

A new C.O. was posted to the Squadron – Johnny Carswell, whom everyone grew to love and respect. The Squadron swopped 'planes with a French squadron and had a grand dog-fight. Our pilots had a hell of a job landing, as the throttles were the opposite way round to ours, and nearly everyone slammed the motor full on just as they were touching down. There were some terrific parties in the evening.

Sergt. 'Dinkie' Powell force-landed one evening 100 yards in Belgium. 'Dinkie' ran like hell, and got pulled through the barbed wire by the French, just as the Belgian frontier guards caught him up. He managed to throw his parachute through first. He said afterwards that he daren't leave that behind, as actually it belonged to Dickie Lylles – another pilot. That night most of 87 massed on the frontier, armed with ropes and a tractor. A plot had been hatched to pull the 'plane across the frontier. Unfortunately, our "spies", consisting of some of the boys in civvies, who sneaked across the frontier and hung about the 'plane, reported that it was guarded by three machine-guns, so they all went back to bed feeling very browned off. Such had been the life of my new Squadron before the blitz.

"Wake up; you're at readiness in half an hour." Hell! It was about three-thirty, and we were to be at readiness by four.

I leapt out of my camp bed; a quick wash, then downstairs, where I met other sleepy pilots snatching a quick breakfast. A hoot from the outside told us that the Citroen van was waiting to take us to the dispersal points on the aerodrome. We bundled in. Cries of, "Wait a moment! Where's 'Watty'?"

'Watty' arrived, running out of the mess half dressed; then off we went down a dirty, cobbly road. The van lurched from side to side as the Flight Sergeant who drove it cursed. The steering was as loose as hell – we seemed to be in a permanent speed wobble.

At last, after a hectic three miles, we turned off the road. "All out for "A" Flight." I scrambled out with 'Watty' and Chris; the van bumped off down the road for "B" Flight.

It was my first day of readiness with 87. It was cool, as the sun had only just appeared over the horizon and was slowly climbing into the cloudless blue sky. We were to do a dawn patrol across the lines towards Brussels. 85 Squadron was to have two sections to meet us over Lille; they were operating from the 'drome south of us.

We wandered to our 'planes. They had already been warmed up. We checked that our parachutes and helmets were handy, then there was nothing to do but wait. We sat by the 'phone; it might ring at any time, giving us patrol orders. Nothing happened. We idly turned the pages of well-thumbed books; several of them were the pornographic literature collected by the boys from the shops of Paris, Amiens and Lille. The sun grew warmer. I asked 'Watty' and Chris how many 'planes they had shot down. Chris told me one – a Heinkel over Valenciennes about a week ago. 'Watty' was like me – nothing.

Gradually, steadily, the time passed. Six o'clock was zero hour. At ten to, the engines were started; we clambered in.

The 'plane I had got only arrived from England the day before – a brand-new one, with the latest variable-pitch rotol airscrew. Already a black cat – my mascot – was painted on its side. We taxied out. On the other side of the aerodrome, we saw "B" Flight turning into wind for the take-off. Soon we roared across the ground. Air-borne, we swung southwards for the centre of the town. Where the hell were 85?

After a few minutes, which seemed to me like hours, three Hurricanes climbed towards us. There seemed to be only nine of us, then. 85 were the leaders. Their section turned eastward; we followed, keeping well up. Looking either side, I saw 'Watty' and Chris weaving;[7] farther across, "B" Flight wing men were doing the same thing. We droned onwards, climbing to 12,000 feet, then levelled out.

---

[7] "Weaving" means that the last 'planes of any formation fly on a twisting, snake-like course. By doing this the pilots can get a view behind them to their right and to their left alternately. This is the only way in which single-seater fighters, which are blind to the rear, can prevent enemy fighters from getting on their tails and shooting them down.

Beneath us the country was looking peaceful; except for patches of fog, the visibility was good. Looking back, Lille shone in the sun. There was nothing to show that there was a war on. Suddenly to our right appeared a black burst, then another; a score sprang into existence. Our formation started evasive action – climbing, diving, twisting and turning. I looked down; there was nothing below that showed me that now we were over the enemy lines. The A.A. was uncannily accurate: whenever we changed height the bursts seemed to follow us, always just a bit behind – just as well for us! Soon we were past the guns, and once more everything looked peaceful.

We droned on. On the R.T. a guttural voice starts talking. Blast these sets! Why can't they keep them tuned? I turn the volume down and move my tuning-arm. Hell! It's German. Wish the hell I could understand the language. It sounds hellishly close. I crane round, searching the sky behind. Nothing, not a cloud even – just steady blue. The weaving of our wing men becomes more vigorous.

In the distance I can see a haze of smoke, steeples and towers. Brussels.

Christ! there they are – five specks coming towards us well below. I waggle my wings, "Line astern, line astern. Go."

Messerschmitt 110s; nine of us against five of them. This looks easy. What the hell are the leading section doing? Still in vic formation, they sail on. 'Well, here goes, boys.' I bank over for a right-hand diving turn. Out of the corner of my eye I see "B" Flight's section, in line astern, wheeling towards us. The enemy are flying in rather a wide vic formation. I decide on the right-hand 'plane, "Echelon port, echelon port. Go." 'Watty' and Chris swing up on my left. They still haven't seen us. We are diving steeply now, doing about 300 on the clock.

'Throttle back a bit; otherwise, you'll overshoot them. Hell! They've broken. What the hell! they have turned to meet us. Steady, now; get your sights on before you fire. Rat tat tat, rat tat tat. Hell!

31

you can hear their cannons firing. Blast it! I am going too fast: they are past me, on either side – so close that I thought we would hit.'

As they pass, their rear-gunners fire at me; their tracer goes over my head.

'A quick left-hand turn. Steady, or you'll black out.'

As I turn, the sky seems full of black crosses; another one overshoots me.

'Hell! they must have dived out of the sky.'

To my right a Hurricane goes down in flames; by it there's a white puff as a parachute opens.

'Keep turning – tighter, tighter. God! they turn badly. I wonder if I'll get out of this alive? Another couple of turns; it's only a question of time before one of those rear-gunners hits me.'

At last I can get my sights on – a full deflection on the inside of the turn. I thumb the firing-button: a tearing noise as my guns fire.

'Got him.'

My bullets hit his petrol tanks, a stream of white vapour pours from his wing tanks, a whouf! almost in my face – his wings on fire. He turns on his back, trailing fire and smoke behind, plunges into a wood below.

'Keep turning.'

My lips crack, my cockpit smells of the oily compressed air that fires my guns.

Only three thousand feet up now. Three of the b------s are at me – seem to be the centre of their circle; their rear-gunners banging away at me. Silly b------s! One of them overshoots me – in front of me; only twenty-five yards' range. Brrrrrrrrr, brrrrrrrrm. God! I can't miss. Brrrrr – a blur of white and black.

My windscreen is covered with muck. I've hit his oil and glycol tank. I still turn tight as I can. A flash from below – that last one has just hit the deck; no parachutes.

'God! I wonder if I am going to get out of this. Not a sight of another Hurricane in the sky. Far above there seem to be a lot of 'planes; these damned Huns are bloody bad at turning.'

A few more turns and one of them is in my sights again. I thumb the gun-button. Nothing happens. I press again.

'Oh, Hell! I am out of ammo.'

A shiver runs down my spine. Still turning as steeply as I possibly can, I dive for the deck.

'Down, down. Thank God they've broken away from me.'

At about 100 feet I straighten up, pull the tit;[8] a jerk as my supercharger goes up to twelve boosts.

'You bloody fool! You're going the wrong way: swing round and head for the sun.' The Jerries must be above me some way away. Oh God, don't let them see me. 'Streak along, dodging trees and houses.' Thank God, another Hurricane's doing the same thing. I'll follow him home.

Just as I am drawing up to formate on this Hurricane, he dips; I catch a fleeting glimpse of flying brick, and, seemingly quite slowly, a Hurricane's tail, with the red, white and blue stripes, flies up past my cockpit. I glance behind, and see a cloud of dust slowly rising.

'Hell! He must have had some bullets in him to hit that house. Wonder who it was? I seem to be the only survivor. Blast these fog patches! Keep going west. Untwist the emergency boost button (the tit)' – boost sinks back to normal. 'Now let's have a look at the map.'

My hands are shaking and my feet are drumming on the floor. I can't stop them.

I'm sweating like a pig. Glancing at the cockpit clock, I see that it is exactly six-thirty; yet the sun seems hellishly hot.

'Oh, I can't make head or tail of these French maps. A town on the left, so sheer off southwards and have a look. It seems quite a big town; but I can't find it on the map. Now keep cool; go westwards for fifteen minutes, then turn north, and you'll hit the coast.'

---

[8] This is the emergency control which, by driving the supercharger at its very maximum pace, gives the aeroplane considerable extra speed. But the strain on the engine is terrific. So, it must only be used in case of need, and then not for long, or the engine may blow up.

At last, after what seemed hours, I saw the coast. Now it was only a case of guessing which way to turn to find an aerodrome. I turned westwards, as I was damned if I wanted to run into any more Huns just yet. Soon I came upon an airfield. For a second, I had a nasty jolt, as the 'planes that I could see looked exactly like Jerry dive-bombers. Immediately I saw the French markings and felt at ease. I circled once, saw the direction of the wind, and came in to land. There were a few bomb-holes on the 'drome; several hangars looked the worse for wear – no roofs and bulging walls. I taxied up to some of the other machines. Several French airmen ran to meet me as I jumped out. God! how lovely it was to be on firm ground again.

Nobody appeared to speak English. I was shepherded to one of the huts by the hangars, where I was greeted in very broken English by a Capitaine, who told me that I was at Berck, near Le Touquet. They shoved me in a car and rushed me off down a dusty road to a small chateau, where it appeared they had their officers' mess; there they rapidly produced for me a colossal breakfast of two eggs and multitudes of rashers of bacon. I did not feel at all hungry, only slightly sick. My hand was shaking so much that the coffee-cup rattled against the saucer, which added to my embarrassment. A rather one-sided conversation went on. I managed to make them understand that I had shot down two Messerschmitts and that I thought my friends had been killed. They told me that they were the fleet air arm, and of late had done several raids on German-occupied Rotterdam.

I managed to borrow a map back at the aerodrome and to show the French crew how to crank the handles to start my Hurricane. She soon started, and off I went. By now the fog had cleared and the country looked green and clear beneath the cloudless sky. Soon the chimneys of Lille hove in sight and I was throttling back for the landing on the aerodrome, which I had left only three hours before. In that time, I had seen death in flaming 'planes, heard the crack of the cannon-shells aimed to kill me, felt fear and exultation, despair and hope, helplessness and strength.

As I taxied in the crews ran to meet me, and, God! can it be true? 'Watty' and Chris were there too. – "How many, sir?" – "Two." – "Damn good shooting, sir." – "Hullo, 'Watty'. How many did you get?" – "One." – "Damned good show. What about Chris?" – "He got a probable; he was having too hot a time to see what happened to it. Whew! it was hot. They fought like hell, the swine. Where the hell have you been, 'Widge'? We thought you were finished. We were just saying, wonder who the new Flight Commander will be."

"Well, old boy, it was like this. I hadn't the remotest idea where I was when I broke off the scrap. I started following another Hurricane; he hit a house, so I pushed off west; then what with fog and French maps I was properly foxed, so after a bit I turned north, hit the coast and landed at a French fleet-air-arm 'drome at Berck. They stuffed me with breakfast, and here I am. I thought that I was the only survivor."

"That's what we thought too. Poor 85 must have lost their boys. I saw two Hurricanes crash definitely. When I left the scrap after my ammo was finished, I saw one 'Hurribox' fighting five Jerries; I was scared stiff that they would come after me."

By the time we had told each other what had happened, the sun was flaming down from a clear blue sky. We took off our tunics and lolled in the heat. The Citroen van rolled up with a pile of pilots to relieve us. We scrambled in, off to the mess for breakfast – a second one as far as I was concerned. The trees looked very green and the world unusually happy; we all thought how good it was to be alive. In the mess we met the C.O. and some of the ground staff; they showered congratulations on us, and made us shoot them a line.

Breakfast tasted good. I managed to eat much more than my first one, which seemed years ago. As soon as we were finished, we had a quick shave, then back to readiness.

Most of the Squadron wore dark blue, soft shirts, bought from the local village; the service type that I had on cut your neck when you craned round to see that nothing was on your tail. It was best to look behind at least four minutes out of every five: most people who had been shot down, and had got back to tell the tale, had said that they never saw what had hit them. I asked 'Chiefy', the flight sergeant, to get a village shirt for me, and in the meantime, I took my collar off.

One of the things that had rather shaken me whilst I was in the mess was that the ginger-haired stores officer, who was mess secretary, had relieved me of 500 francs for the mess fund. He explained that everyone gave that, just in case they didn't come back. This was the real thing – war.

When we got back to the Flight nothing had happened, but orders had come through that the Squadron was to do a patrol over Brussels, leaving at 13.00 hours; Johnny, the C.O., would lead the second section of three, with David Rhodes; "B" Flight covering our tails. The whole of the morning was all quiet on the Western Front (but where the front was nobody seemed to know). The operations room, which was located in a barn, rang us up about once per hour to give us synchronized time – other than that everything was peaceful.

Four or five of the boys had a pontoon school going on the grass; others sat around in the deck-chairs and discussed leave, girls, what we should do that evening – on the whole, just binding gently, or now and then calling to the orderly for another cup of tea. A kettle was always kept on the primus. Tea was a franc a cup, and the tea swindlers were reported to be making a fortune and buying a café in the town.

The telephone rang; it was the orders to start up for Brussels. We ran to our machines, clambered in, shouts of "Contact," and the men cranked the handles, the engines spluttered, then roared, and we were off. The Squadron formed up and swung eastwards; the chimneys of Lille disappeared in the haze; the red roofs of Tourney to the south of us looked like a peaceful English town. I flew on a steady course, keeping well up on Johnny and some way out to his right. My wing men, 'Watty' and Saunders, crossed and re-crossed, weaving behind me. Behind us Mitchell's section weaved 1,000 feet above us, protecting our tails. I felt somehow safe, although I had the usual sinking feeling, just as I used to have before a boxing match at school. We had climbed to 12,000 feet and flew steadily along towards the smudge in the distance which was Brussels.

Suddenly on the R.T. came, "Messerschmitts above us." Up in the blue I saw two specks; now and then they glinted in the sun as they twisted and turned.

"Hullo, Red one. Break away and attack with your section." – 'Hell! that was me; well, here goes!'

I opened up to nearly full throttle, climbing steeply.

'Blast them! Come down, you.'

Below, the Squadron was just reaching the outskirts of the city; above us the 109s were climbing and flying eastwards. Damn this for a joke! At this rate we would never catch them – at least, not until we were well in enemy territory. I thought of them calling up their colleagues on their R.T., saying, "Come up and get them; here are three English suckers." – 'Blast! I'll chuck it.'

I throttled back and dived down to rejoin the Squadron. We patrolled up and down for about half an hour without seeing a thing, then turned for home. We got back and landed without seeing another 'plane. A crowd of us dashed off to the mess for lunch, while the men refuelled the 'planes, bashing holes in the four-gallon tins and slopping the petrol in the tanks. It was a good lunch on a bright red, chequered table-cloth – stew, potatoes and salad. Then cheese, biscuits and some bloody stuff which was a mixture of margarine and butter. It tasted foul; pure margarine is far better. Nearly all of us drank light beer or orange squash and water.

My blue shirt had arrived – thirty-five francs' worth. I rapidly changed into it, and felt much cooler; in the sun it was flaming hot. Back to dispersal, where we sat and waited. There was no activity at all. Then orders came through for a wing[9] sweep to take place at 21.00 hours, destination secret.

---

[9] That is, a sweep of a whole Wing (three Squadrons or thirty-six aircraft) flying together.

We sat and waited. Still nothing happened. Soon it was getting on for evening; the sun had lost most of its heat. "Ops" 'phoned up and gave us the "gen"[10] on the raid. It was to be a bombing raid on Namur. We were to escort fifteen Blenheims – rendezvous over Lille at 5,000.

"Your job is to see the bombers get through; you are not to be diverted away from them, whatever happens. Do not get involved in a dog-fight." Blast that for a joke. Well, here goes. Once more we taxied out to take off – not only us: this time there would be thirty-six of us. We took off. After a slight shambles, when half the Squadron chased Sergeant Bowell, thinking he was Johnny, our C.O., who was to lead us, we got into proper formation.[11]

We were leading the fighter formation – by far the best position. We picked the bombers up on time and set off. It was a glorious evening, with a flaming western sky. Just past Mons the sky suddenly became full of ack ack burst. Damned accurate, too – dead right height, but on the whole too far behind. But not too far; as I glanced behind, I saw one of the arse-end Hurricanes plummet out of the sky, a black trail behind it. I saw a black dot, then a puff of white as the pilot's parachute opened. Poor devil! he would land in Jerry territory. The sky behind was full of black puffs. No new ones burst: we were through the ack ack barrage.

On we droned. Out of the corner of my eye I saw nine dots high above us. 'Hell! Jerries.' All of a sudden about five people were speaking at the same time on the R.T.; the weaving at the back became fiercer than ever. 'Hell! what the devil does that section think it's doing?' Right at the back of the formation one section of three was flying in close vic formation, as though they were doing a show for the Hendon air pageant.

---

[10] "Gen" means information. Derivation: "genuine information", contracted to "genuine"; contracted to "gen." The word carries some, but not all, of the implications of "low down on" or "inside dope".

[11] It is by no means difficult to mistake one aircraft for another in these, and other, circumstances.

Even as I craned round, I saw three of the black dots swinging behind us come diving down. 'Hell, blast! What the hell can we do?' Another babble of voices on the R.T. Too late – the sky was suddenly lit up by two burning Hurricanes. Down, down; a trail of smoke on the ground; no one had baled out.

The attacking 109s had dived beneath and were heading for home at a rough 450 m.p.h. The other six still hung about well above. The complete Squadron at the back was weaving violently. On we flew. I had a dry, unpleasant taste in my mouth. Soon below us we could see the airfield that we had come to bomb. The bomber boys did their stuff well: huge columns of smoke rose from the 'drome, and soon several of the aerodrome buildings were burning fiercely.

We turned, heading into the setting sun. I felt slightly ill. Away to the south of us a town was burning – it was the first sign of the war on the ground that I had seen; a long wave of dirty smoke rolled across the countryside. Looking at the map, I guessed it to be Mezières. It was an ugly sight, and it sent a cold shiver down my back. The setting sun was a glorious sight. "Red sky at night, shepherd's delight."

Over Lille we split up and wheeled down to land in quick succession. Only about another hour at readiness, then supper and bed. God! I felt tired.

Back at the mess, after a quick drink most of us retired to our camp beds. No sooner had I clambered in than crack, crack-bang, crash-wallop, wallop; the whole house shook: the Jerries were giving Lille a smart blitz. Frankly I lay in bed and literally shivered with fear. This was the bitter end. The bombing kept up for about three hours. I didn't know the difference between the A.A. guns and bombs, so I was perpetually frightened. My usual outlook of Kismet – if you are going to be hit by a bomb you will be – had deserted me. Eventually I dropped off in an uneasy slumber.

'Dimmy' Deacon woke me at six; we were to be at readiness at six-thirty. This time "B" Flight were doing the dawn patrol. A quick shave in cold water and a hasty but fruitless search for my little gold

St. Christopher mascot, which always hung round my neck. I turned the place upside down, but couldn't find it. This, I thought, was the end. I didn't at all relish flying without it.

I missed breakfast by searching for it, so drove the Citroen van down the road at a hell of a bat, feeling sick and unhappy. When we arrived at dispersal, we heard that the dawn patrol had knocked down a lone Heinkel, which presumably had been doing a recco[12] flight.

Along the road past the aerodrome a trickle of refugees were passing. After a few hours this trickle grew into a steady stream, some in cars with mattresses slung on the roof, the majority on bicycles, with their worldly goods tied to the handle-bars, a few on foot, pushing prams piled high with blankets, clothes and food.

It was another glorious day, with the sun streaming down from the cloudless blue sky. We lay about in our shirt-sleeves, now and then wandering over to the road to try to talk to the refugees. We gathered that most of them were Belgians, and, according to them, the Jerries were thirty kilometres behind them, being held by a handful of British and French troops.

There was a feeling of unrest in the air. We 'phoned Ops[13] and asked them if they had any dope, but they couldn't tell us a thing – their plotting system had broken down. We soon had proof of this. Two Lysanders were circling the aerodrome at about 2,000 feet, presumably coming in to land. Suddenly out of the sky dived nine specks.

As soon as we saw them, we heard the rat-a-tat of their cannons. "Start up! start up!" we yelled as we ran to our 'planes. My engine was running as I reached my 'plane. "Damn the straps! get off!" I screamed at the crew. I slammed the throttle open and tore across the ground for a cross-wind take-off, just missing a 'plane that appeared from my left. I slammed the wheels up and looked up.

---

[12] Reconnaissance.

[13] Operations.

Two black trails of smoke hung over the wood just by the 'drome; one man was swinging slowly down on his parachute; the nine 109s were diving eastwards, about 1,000 yards in front of me, being closely followed by two Hurricanes. I had been quick off the deck, but somebody had been quicker. I shoved the throttle, trying to get it farther forward.

'Damn! We're flat out as it is. Here goes with the tit.' A jerk – the boost's shot up to twelve pounds; speed's increased by 30 m.p.h. I'm gaining ground – 700, 600, 500 yards. Give him a burst. No, hold your fire, you fool! he hasn't seen you yet. 400, 300 yards. Now steady, sights on. Right, here goes. Brrrrrrrrrrrm! Got him.'

He dived down, and I thought he was going straight in the deck, but he pulled out, missing a wood by what looked like inches to me. By now I was about 200 yards behind him.

'Another burst. Got him this time. There's a dirty trail of black smoke coming from his engine, a splash of oil on my windscreen. Another burst and another. Blast this for a joke! Where the hell am I getting to? Brmmmmm, brmmmmm. A puff of white – that would be his glycol tank. Get down, damn you!'

Twice he looked exactly as if he was going to hit a house or some wires; a village flashed past me; out of the corner of my eye I saw a machine-gun post firing at me. 'Hell to this!' Brmmmmm, brmmmmm. Then just a hiss. 'Hell, I'm out of ammo!'

The 109 was going much slower – doing a bare 200, with clouds of smoke pouring from him; he was about 50 feet off the deck. I whipped into a steep right-hand turn, released the boost tit, and hared for home, hedge-hopping.

Then I nearly had heart failure: a formation of five 109s passed straight over me going the other way only about 3000 feet up. I was sweating like a pig. Suddenly in a green field I saw khaki soldiers waving at me. Thank God I was across the line! Whew, my knees felt shaky! I did a bumpy landing and taxied in.

My crew ran up. "How many, sir?" "One? damn good show!" I clambered out. Robbie strolled up. "Any luck, old boy?" I told him.

"Good show! I got one too – down in flames." We went into the tent to fill in the combat reports – a sort of questionnaire on a green sheet. I discovered, to my annoyance, that I should only be able to claim mine as a probable, as I hadn't seen it hit the deck. I cursed, but there wasn't a hope in hell of getting it confirmed, as it was miles the wrong side of the lines. Blast! Still, I was quite sure that he didn't get home. One of the 504 boys had got one too.

We weren't on the ground long. From the end of the aerodrome a red Verey soared up; we sprinted to our 'planes – it was the emergency signal, meaning every 'plane off the ground. We slammed the throttles open; 'planes were taking off in every direction, the Rotol airscrew 'planes getting off first, scraping over the variable-pitch models, who in turn soared over the wooden prop versions.[14]

I was petrified, heaving at the stick to get some height. Up in the sky ack ack bursts showed where the Jerries were. There were about thirty bombers, with showers of fighters. I was fairly well in front of about fifty Hurricanes, climbing flat out. The Jerries saw us coming and swung round eastwards. 'Good show!' I thought – 'at least we've turned them back.' We were all gaining on them. Behind me I saw some of the 109s dive at the straggling "Hurries".

A dog-fight developed. We in front climbed upwards; the bombers, for some unknown, foolish reason, started breaking formation and

---

[14] The fixed wooden airscrew, the variable-pitch airscrew, and the Rotol constant-speed airscrew, represent three important stages in the development of operational aircraft. The effect of the change-over from a fixed airscrew to one of variable pitch is to enable the pilot to alter the "set" of his propeller, much as an oarsman feathers his blade. Thus, he will take off with the blade in "fine", so that it presents only a narrow surface to the air as it revolves. Therefore, it spins round at a very high speed, giving the aircraft the most rapid possible take off – much as a low gear enables a car to accelerate to the maximum. Then, when the aircraft is flying, the pilot changes the set of the propeller to "coarse" – like an oarsman's blade in the water. This has the same effect as changing a car into top gear.

The Rotol constant-speed airscrew is a further, and remarkable, development of this device. In aircraft fitted with it the number of revolutions of the engine per minute is actually kept constant, for, when the throttle is opened and the engine gives more power, the airscrew automatically goes into coarser pitch, so that the extra power merely maintains the same number of revolutions and drives the aircraft faster.

dispersing in all directions. I had my eye on a Heinkel 111 which had separated itself and was some way away from the protecting Jerry fighters. I was soon up to him, aimed carefully and gave him a short burst; a stream of smoke from his port engine. I was closing rapidly now, sights on again; this time I gave him a long burst.

'Hell! everything has gone black: His whole oil-tank must have burst. Slam the hood open. All over the wings the oil glistens. Hell! I'm nearly ramming him.'

I shove the stick forward and just miss his tail. As I passed, a black object flashed past my cockpit; a puff of white as a parachute opened. The Heinkel fell away to my left, going down in a gentle, ever-increasing spiral. He hit the ground in the centre of a large wood and blew up with a terrific flash; chunks of wood and flaming debris drifted up towards me. I turned to see where the parachutist had got to; he had just landed in what appeared to be an empty field. In a matter of seconds, the field was full of sprinting men, some soldiers and some civvies; the parachutist disappeared under a crowd of people.

As soon as I had landed, the crew were asking the usual question: they knew from the oil on my machine that I had got something. Robbie also got one of the Heinkels, and several of the other chaps had shot down 109s. So far Jackson, the Australian, and 'Joycey' weren't back.

After an hour we 'phoned Ops, and, as they had no news, reported them missing. Jackson we never heard of again; Joyce landed, with his wheels up, with half a leg blown off by cannon-fire. Some French soldiers looked after him and got him back to hospital at Amiens, where he had his leg amputated. Of course, we didn't hear those details for some days, so to us they were just missing. One bullet-hole was found in my machine; it had just missed the petrol tank.

No sooner was the oil cleaned off, and the machine rearmed and refuelled, than there was another panic take-off. This time I was first off the deck. I saw a mass of Jerries in close formation over

Lille, which they were bombing heavily; the usual fighter escort was weaving above them.

'Blast them! they were dropping a packet. God! you are swines. There's nothing in the town itself except thousands and thousands of refugees. Come on, boys.'

I glanced back at the crowd of Hurricanes behind me. 'Hell! wish I wasn't in front. Blast you b-----s! you've dropped your dirt. We'll smash you before you get home.' I was gaining on them quickly. 'God! what marvellous formation flying.' The bombers sailed through the sky, their metal-work glinting. High above, the protecting fighters darted here and there. 'If they come down, there's going to be a hell of a party. Damn! Don't shoot now, you fools!' Black anti-aircraft bursts appeared unpleasantly close to us; as usual, behind and below the bombers: the bursts were just about landing in the middle of the pursuing Hurricanes.

'On; not much farther. The return fire is going to be bloody hot. Now, don't be a fool: wait until some of the others catch up before you close.' I throttled back a bit and did a quick weave. High above, the escort fighters looked like skylarks; they seemed to show no signs of coming down to attack us. The left-hand back one will do me nicely. 'Waste your ammo; you won't hit me yet.' The whole formation was pouring tracer bullets at us.

'Here goes, full throttle again. Sights on. Close a bit. Steady. Now – Brrrrrrmmmm. Got him! A huge flash; the starboard engine is blazing furiously. Go down, damn you! Brrrrrrrmmm.'

The Dornier sailed on, still in close formation, his whole wing burning; even in the sun the flames seemed bright. Then suddenly it toppled on to its side and just dropped from the sky. 'Look behind, look behind,' the warning voice inside me was screaming. I glanced behind. 'Hell! 109s. Let's get out of this, quick. Blast you!' A Hun was just about dead on my tail. Out of the corner of my eye I saw the massive formation splitting, with several bombers spiralling down. But two 109s seemed to have picked on me. Around me a gigantic dog-fight was taking place; it was impossible to see which was friend or foe until you were close enough to see the aircraft markings. Round and round I went. Slowly but steadily, I was turning inside the 109. Round and round until I felt sick and hardly knew which way up I was. Now and then I flashed by other 'planes, sometimes with black crosses and sometimes with roundels.

'You're a stubborn swine – a few more turns and you'll have had it.' Damn! it was as if the Hun had heard my thoughts. He turned on his back and dived vertically. I followed. Brrrrrrmmmm. Damn! that was a shaky shot. Christ! a large chunk of something flew off. A snaky white trail suddenly appeared by my cockpit. 'Someone on your tail; aileron turn, quick. Stick hard over to one side. That's lost him. Thank God for that! Now for home.'

I searched the sky. The bombers had beat it, closely followed by fleeing 109s. I roared low over several burning wrecks. I was soon at the 'drome, and landed quickly. What a morning! It was only mid-day, but I felt as if it was late evening. I had got five. How long can this go on? All my boys were back safely. Robbie had knocked a Dornier down and had about twenty bullet-holes in his 'plane. The others had only inconclusive scraps with the 109s.

The Intelligence blokes went into Lille to see if they could find anything worth having from any of the crashed. We piled into the Citroen and hurtled off for some lunch. Nearly everyone that we met had got something down that morning. A lot of shop was talked at lunch. We were all very cheerful. We had lost three pilots. Nobody talked about that. I managed to scribble a letter to Pam and home, saying that all was well and that my score was mounting.

Then back to readiness. As we drove along the road this time half the British army seemed to be on it, straggling along in single file. We stopped and asked one of the blokes what the hell they were doing. They said they were retreating. Hell! we thought, that wasn't so funny. There was still a pile of refugees. Things didn't look so good.

As we sat at dispersal the stream of army increased; quite a lot of them were hanging on to lorries and Bren-gun carriers. They repeated the refugee's story that Jerry had a Panzer division five miles up the road. We dismissed these ideas as fifth-columnist rumours. A rumour was also going round that half the French generals had been given the sack, and that Gamelin was reported to be the head of the Fifth Column in France.

Our men began to get uneasy. They jokingly asked how the hell they were going to get away if the Jerries appeared. They joked, but it was obvious that they were worried. Very few of them had rifles, the others had just nothing. Ops were getting worried too. They gave orders that the Squadron was to get ready to move at half an hour's notice. So down came our tent and everything that could be piled high on lorries.

Nobody seemed to know where the front line was, or what the hell was happening. Still the army went by. A large convoy of ambulances passed, full of wounded. The war seemed to be getting very close to us.

Chapter 5

The End of France

That afternoon we sat and waited. Everything seemed very quiet. Along the road more and more army straggled, the sun beating piteously down on their sweating forms. We lay in our shirt-sleeves, sunbathing and chatting quietly, watching the road and wondering what the hell was happening. Now and then a section or flight of 'planes took off, and returned having seen nothing.

Tea-time came along. We were just arguing whose turn it was to go first, when one of the crews shouted that there was a 'plane in flames. There it was over Lille, very high. As we looked it came plummeting down, trailing a dirty black streak behind; at about 20,000 feet there was a puff of white as a parachute opened. A cloud of dust rose from the ground where the 'plane had hit; high above we could see the tiny white canopy bringing its pilot slowly down to safety. "Theirs or ours?" Whoever it was, he was going to have a long ride down, and would eventually land fairly near us, as there was a gentle wind blowing our way.

I rushed off to tea with my section, 'Watty' and Banks. Tea tasted good. The batmen had fantastic rumours that the Jerries had broken through south of us. They told us that the village behind the mess was practically deserted. Back to dispersal to relieve the others for tea. When we arrived there about forty minutes after we had left, the parachutist was still about 5,000 feet, and looked as if he would land slap in the middle of Lille. Ops had 'phoned us and said that it was one of ours – a 504 bloke who had been shot down by a 109.

We still sat around and waited. Things weren't so comfortable now, as most of our comforts were piled high on the lorries, waiting for the move to Heaven knows where.

At about six the 'phone rang. The Squadron was to move to Merville immediately. Hell, and damnation! We hoped that our batmen had packed our kit O.K. "Well, here goes, boys. Cheerio, 'Chiefy'; we'll see you at Merville." It wasn't too big a move, as Merville was only 40 miles behind Lille. It took us a bare fifteen minutes to fly there.

We arrived over the aerodrome in company with another Squadron. The ground seemed covered with aircraft already. Where we were meant to go nobody seemed to know. We taxied round the 'drome trying to find somewhere to put our 'planes. At last, we found a corner – not too far away from a café, we noted. Several of the boys knew Merville well, as they had been stationed there earlier in the war.

There we were, with no men to start us up, even. We got the starter handles out and arranged to start each other up. We had left one of our "Hurryboxes" back at Lillemark. It was 'Watty's' old "G", which had had its control wires and main longerons shot away that morning; the tail was just about falling off. We hoped to send a crew back to fix it up; we never saw "G" again.

Dusk began to fall just as our lorries arrived. Thank God they had arrived, anyway. Where we, or they, were going to sleep that night nobody knew. The Doc arrived in his car, so 'Watty' and I went into the village to find some billets for the men, and for ourselves. 'Doc' Curry was damned good at French, which helped a lot. After a lot of arguing we eventually found the key of the school-house, so commandeered that. Everywhere else was crammed full of refugees; we managed to oust some of these from part of the little cinema, and put the rest of the men there. Now where the hell were we going? That seemed a different matter.

Actually, I had already found myself a bed, in one of the houses next to the 'drome – a huge double bed. All I was worrying about now was my tummy, which felt very empty. A crowd of us wandered along to the café at the cross-roads; it was full of soldiers and local inhabitants. After a spot of arguing we managed to get them to produce big plates of bacon and eggs; this went down damned well with plenty of beer. We had found several old friends at Merville, who were in the other Squadrons there. Eventually I wandered down the road with young Banks, with whom I had offered to share my room.

He was a young boy who was looking very tired. He had come out three days before, having ferried a new Hurricane over to us. God knows where our luggage was; we didn't bother about that. After asking the lady of the house to wake us at four-thirty, we retired to our room with a couple of candles, stripped and leapt into bed naked. When the candles were blown out, I lay in bed and thought. Oh hell! I suddenly remembered that I hadn't told anyone where we were sleeping. I hope she wakes us. My thoughts wandered. In two minutes, I was asleep.

We were woken punctually. It was a filthy morning, pouring with rain. We were cheered by hot coffee and a couple of boiled eggs, which were waiting for us as soon as we had struggled into our clothes. There seemed to be nowhere to wash, so we just didn't bother. We thanked Madame very much, and after a difficult few moments, gave her fifty francs for our lodgings. She didn't want to take anything, but we insisted.

We wandered out to the tin Nissen hut which was our dispersal hut. Only a few pilots were there; God knows where the others were. The bell rang: two 'planes to take off and patrol Arras. Dennis Knight and Robbie went off. The rest of us sat shivering in the hut, listening to the rain drumming on the tin roof. Within half an hour they were back. Robbie had seen nothing. Dennis Knight landed pleased as Punch – he had shot down a Junkers 88. One of his wings had five bullet-holes in it, one slap through the oil-tank. He was damned lucky to get back. It was his first Hun.

A few minutes of peace, then the 'phone again: two more aircraft to take off and patrol Arras. "You are to keep a careful eye out for dive-bombers."

Dick Lyle and I decided to go. We got soaked as we ran to our 'planes. We got off the ground after rushing through showers of liquid mud. We swung south, both weaving gently; a dark smudge on the horizon showed us our destination. Some Jerries had done their work already: the station and several large buildings were burning; a dirty black column of smoke rose from some of them. We flew up and down; nothing happened.

After half an hour the weather began to clear a bit; after an hour the sun was shining from a clear sky; a few clouds sailed by, blown by a strong south-westerly wind. I sat aching in my cockpit, wishing that something would happen, feeling empty in the tummy. It was eight o'clock, and I thought that I could do with some breakfast. My thoughts of food were interrupted by Dick, who flashed by me waggling his wings frantically. I craned my neck and looked behind. Nothing. Hell! there they were – about twelve Junkers 88, sailing along towards us. Without an escort, too.

'Blast! They've seen us; they're turning back. What bloody fools! They're breaking formation. Here goes!'

I slammed the throttle wide open and went for the nearest 'plane. Out of the corner of my eye I saw Dick going in to attack. Blast him! my bloke was diving and diving, damned fast. I got him in my sights. 'Blast! 500 yards – too far; and he's going away from me. Going down, 8, 7, 6, 5, 4,000 feet. Here goes with the tit.'

A jerk as I jump forward with the added power. 'That's better; now I'm catching him. Down, down we go – right down to ground-level. Damn you!' The rear-gunner gave me a burst which was too close to me for comfort.

'Right; 250 yards now. Careful. Brrrrmmmmm, brrrmmm. Damn that rear gunner! Brmmmmm – that'll fix you; brmmmmm, brmmmmmm, brmmmmmmmmmmm. Get down, damn you! Hell! he has.'

A cloud of dust and debris flew up past my cockpit. 'Whew, that was a close one!' He must have had his bomb-load on: there was a large hole where he had crashed. No survivors from that one. 'Now, where the hell am I? Blast!'

A shower of pom-pom shells flew up and just missed me – evidently 'not in friendly territory'. I zigzagged violently, climbing hard. Every machine-gun in the district was firing at me; behind me a shower of shells exploded. This was too hot. I climbed flat out. Up at 5,000 things seemed a little quieter. Were they? Like hell! I was looking at the deck, trying to make out where I was, when I heard 'rat-tat-tat'. 'Christ! 109s – five of them.' I pulled the stick back in my tummy and promptly blacked out.[15]

Through the haze I saw something flash past me. As soon as I could see I turned on my back and spiralled down, pulling out at the last moment. Looking over my shoulder, I saw them coming in for another attack. Rat-tat-tat. Hell! this was the end. God! I just missed a tree. 'Look out, you fool! you can't look behind at this height. Oh God, get me out of this.'

Out of the corner of my eye I saw a canal with steep banks. 'Here goes – I can't stay here steep-turning for ever.' I whipped over on the other bank and raced for the canal, hugging the earth so close that I thought my prop would hit. I dived down the embankment, down to water level. A shower of spray went up round me; bullets splashing in the water. 'Thank God! a turn in the canal.'

I whistled round the corner; then another. This was better. I glanced behind me as I went round the second turn. The leading 109 was just in sight. Another turn in front; round that one, then a long straight. 'This is the end. Christ! the engine's packing' – a cough, a splutter, then nothing. 'Gravity tank, you fool, quick!' I turned the cock over: another cough from the engine, then a series of jerks. 'Christ! what the hell's the matter? Look back – sky empty. Now where the hell am

---

[15] 'Black-out' – loss of consciousness by pulling too quickly out of a dive or turning too suddenly.

I? Ah, thank God, there's Lille over to the right. Climb to a thousand. Engine's vibrating and coughing badly. Shall I land at Seclan? Hell! no, it was evacuated yesterday – the Jerries are very likely there. Whew! I wonder how much farther this damned 'plane will carry me?'

I peered over my shoulder anxiously – nothing in sight. Well, now it seems only a case of how long the motor's going to run; all the temperatures were very high – in fact, "emergency only", as the engine manuals put it. 'Come on, old dear, only another twenty miles or so.' I was lucky it wasn't farther, for the main tanks were absolutely dry and my gravity tank had about twenty gallons left. At last, I saw the square wood at the north of the 'drome – Merville at last. I went straight in to land.

Bump, bump, bump, and I was down – hardly a good landing; anyway, I had arrived. Thank God for mother earth!

As soon as I clambered out of my 'plane I saw Dick, pleased as Punch – he had got one, too. I felt damned pleased with life. The weather was looking better too: the clouds were broken and showed signs of dispersing. "What about some breakfast, blokes?" There were crowds of blokes now; many of them had only just arrived, after uncomfortable nights in haystacks and barns; they had gone into Merville for something to eat, and recommended a café to us.

We crowded into the Citroen, 'Watty', Robbie and I in the front, John Banks, Dennis Knight, and Jimmy Smallwood in the back. We were a cheery crowd.

We soon found a place where they would give us eggs and bacon, and – what luxury! – a bath. We crowded upstairs to the one bathroom and tossed up who should have the hot bath. Dennis won; he deserved it, as he had slept in a none-too-clean barn. The rest of us took turns in shaving with the one razor. After three people had been in the bath the water was black, so we drained it off, and turned on the water again. This time it was only lukewarm; still, better than nothing. Dickie Lyle had slept on top of a haystack, and was suffering from a bad cold and hay-fever. By the time he got the bath it was stone cold.

As soon as we were dry and dressed, we crowded down to the café. Except for Madame, the owner, and her rather attractive daughter, it was empty. Madame gossiped to us as she laid the table, and showed us picture postcards of what Merville looked like after the last war. "Were the Bosches near?" – "Who could say?" They said that they were packing up and leaving by the mid-day train. The food arrived, with wizard coffee: it looked, and was, delicious. As we were sipping our coffee Madame reappeared with a huge Alsatian and asked us to shoot it, because they could not take it with them. We were very sorry for them, but none of us had the heart to shoot their dog.

When we went outside the sun was shining, the streets were crowded with the usual refugees, intermingled with quite a crowd of French troops moving forward. Thank God for that! we thought. Some heavy tanks rumbled along the road, eventually stopping behind a horse and cart and causing a terrific jam. We joined in the hooting. At last, the horse and cart were backed into a yard, and the traffic started. Motor-cycles darted in and out, dashing all over the road and pavements, throwing up clouds of dust. By careful weaving we reached the road to the 'drome: back to readiness.

We sat about wondering where our mess was going to be. Several of the boys talked about a convent they had used as a mess when they had been stationed here at the beginning of the war. They said it was a dreary locality – flat, agricultural fields. The 'phone rang: "Keep a good look-out for Huns, as our plotting system has failed again."

Whenever they said that something invariably happened. This time was no exception. No sooner had we posted our look-out than there were yells of "Start up"; drowned by crump, crump, crump. I sprinted out. High above us sailed about twelve bombers in close formation.

As I reached my 'plane the engine started, the crew leapt out. I screamed to them, "Run for it!" Out of the corner of my eye I saw them vanish in the ditch. I slammed the throttle open; I crouched in the cockpit, expecting a bomb to hit me any second.

As my machine gathered speed a couple went off just in front of me. I swerved violently and bounced into the air. Behind me roared three other "Hurries" – only four of us. Up, up. 'Blast the bombers! They're turning south. Up, up. Soon we'll be in range. The left-hand back one would suit me.' I saw the other boys swing out to my right. I got the sights on for a climbing deflection shot; I gave him a burst, then had a quick look behind. 'Oh God! look out, you fool.'

Out of the sky were diving scores of black dots; even as I watched I saw the Hurricane on my right burst into flames; another "Hurry" was diving vertically with two M.E. 110s on its tail. A cold shudder ran down my back; I rolled over and screamed down, aileron turning, down, down; started pulling out.

Everything went grey as I nearly blacked out. I levelled out and looked up. High above me the bombers sailed peacefully on, the M.Es. waltzing here and there behind them. My feet were drumming on the floor of the cockpit. I felt very sick and hot. I weaved violently and headed back to base.

After landing, I found that young Banks and Jimmy Smallwood were missing. The other bloke who got back safely was 'Dimmy' Deacon: he had seen them just in time. The bombs that had dropped had done no damage, except to make a few holes in the 'drome. Robbie was rather shaken, as he was sitting in his cockpit, his crew winding the handles, frantically trying to get the engine to start. Every time a bomb landed, the crew went flat on their faces.

Eventually he chucked it, leapt out and jumped for the ditch. But this particular ditch housed a muddy, slow-running stream, and some of the more particular of the men were lying in it cross-ways, making a bridge of their bodies to keep them out of the water. Robbie landed feet first on top of someone's back, causing the man to go flat on his face in the liquid mud. Everybody thought it was a hell of a joke, except the unfortunate bridge.

The telephone screamed again: "87 Squadron is to take off and ground-straff the Panzer division that is advancing up the Arras Road;

after that the Squadron will evacuate to England." Hell's bells! how many 'planes can we raise? Nine.

"O.K., 'Widge', you lead," said the C.O. "I've got to fix some transport for the ground staff to get away."

"O.K., sir. We'll go over at fifteen thousand and try to dive down out of the sun. Keep a damned good look-out for Jerries. Hell! Robbie, this is hell."

We took off, and soon formed up in three sections of three, the wing men weaving fiercely. We climbed slowly up, heading for Arras.

The sky was dotted here and there with small white clouds; otherwise, it was the azure blue of the previous days. Over to our left appeared a black dot; it was a M.E. 110, which proceeded to fly parallel with us, presumably trailing us. "Hullo, Blue 2 and 3! Break off and fix that 'plane on our left." I looked behind. Blue section was still weaving as previously. 'Blast this wireless!'

On we flew. Arras was in front of us. Clouds of black smoke were towering up from crimson flames from burning buildings – a strangely beautiful yet fearful sight. I looked behind. 'Hell! I'm alone. Where the hell are the boys?' The only 'plane in sight was the M.E. 110; I could just imagine him calling up his colleagues on the R.T. Westwards of the town a smallish cloud hung in the sky. I went flat out for it; so, did the Messerschmitt. Soon I was enveloped in its foggy whiteness.

'Now what the hell shall I do? I am just about at this blasted road that we are meant to straff, but I am all by myself, and very likely half the Luftwaffe are waiting for me. Still, while I'm here I might just as well have a crack at it, so here goes.'

I gingerly climbed up, breaking from the gloom of the cloud to dazzling sunlight shining on the whiteness. 'On my right nothing; Hades! on my left a M.E. 110 about a hundred yards away.' We both shoved the stick forward and disappeared into the cloud: my trailer seemed to be just as windy as I was. Perhaps his R.T. wouldn't work either. 'I'll try going out at the bottom this time.' I closed the throttle and glided down; out in the open I came. 'Whew! slam in front of me there's the M.E. 110. Sights on. Give him a burst. Here goes – brrrrmmm. That'll shake you.' The next second he had gone, up in the cloud again: I bet he wasn't feeling too good.

Now for the ground-straff. I went down to 5,000 and flew along the dead-straight road, which seemed very empty. Was it, though? Under the trees that lined it something was moving, something that looked rather like an evil black snake. 'Well, here goes.' I half rolled on my back and screamed down, thumbing the gun-button as my sights came on the black dots, which rapidly turned into tanks. I roared along the line, pulling out just in time to miss the tall poplar trees. Sssssssss. 'Christ! out of ammo – home, James, and don't spare the horses.' I glanced behind.

A shower of pom-pom shells were bursting just behind my tail. There was a crack, and the 'plane shuddered: a large hole had appeared in my right wing, just outside the petrol tank. I roared over Arras, dodging the houses, many of them battered; past the flaming, smoking station, northwards for Merville, going flat out all the way. God! what a relief it was to see that square wood just north of the 'drome again.

As I went round the circuit, I saw a "Hurrybox" on its nose. It was 'Dimmy's' old J: he had tried to do one of his usual forced-landing approaches, held off too high, and ended up on his nose. Exit the last wooden-prop Hurricane in the Squadron.

Now what the hell had happened to the rest of the boys? I soon found out. 'Watty', who had been flying next to me, had had a complete engine cut. He broke away from the formation and turned for home; his engine came on a bit then, so he dived for home, followed by the rest of the boys, who thought that Messerschmitts were raining out of the sky. When they got back to the 'drome they realised that something was very wrong, so 'Watty' landed and the rest of the boys started off once more to straff the road. Most of them were back, but Robbie and 'Dusty' Miller hadn't landed yet. The others had seen a few tanks. 'Mitch' had managed to cause a traffic jam by setting what must have been an ammo-wagon on fire. He said the occupants leaped out, followed by a shower of fireworks from their lorry, which set the lorry behind it on fire.

A roar of engines – Robbie and 'Dusty' were back. Robbie rolled lazily on his back – the first victory roll that anyone had done in my Flight; and, as far as I could prevent them, it was the last. A victory roll is one of the damn silly traditions that get about. It is really highly dangerous: after a combat it is quite impossible for the pilot to know whether his 'plane is badly damaged or not. If it has got a few bullets in any of the main spars, that victory roll may be the last thing that he does. Still, we were very pleased with Robbie, for he had got a M.E. 110 confirmed in flames and damaged another one.

In our absence orders had come through for the ground crews to pile into the transports and make for Boulogne; the pilots would leave that evening. Christ, what a flap! The transport that we had got was barely sufficient to hold the men; there was absolutely no room for any tool-kits or private luggage of any sort. That meant good-bye to all our clothes. The men were most amusing about that; they began to undress, throwing the clothes they were wearing all over the place and putting on their best tunics. To this day I can see distinctly 'Chiefy'[16] N., stripped naked, putting on clean pants and socks and a spotless clean tunic.

We, the pilots, were hopping about trying to find where the hell our stuff was. Nobody had seen our batmen. We sent out a couple of the men to search the houses and barns. At last, most of the luggage was found in a huge barn full of hay. We took turns to go to the barn and try to pile some of our stuff into towels so that we could shove it into our 'planes. After much scrambling about, I found my large

---

[16] 'Chiefy' means a Flight Sergeant. There is a Flight Sergeant as N.C.O. in charge of each of the two Flights of a Squadron, and another in charge of the Maintenance Flights which do the vital repair work. The Flight Sergeants are some of the most important people in the Squadron.

leather suitcase – one that my mother had given me for my twenty-first birthday present. Of course, the batman had the keys! I found a spade and with Dickie's help smashed the locks. He was hellishly annoyed, because, being a New Zealander, everything that he had in Europe was in two trunks, and there wasn't a hope in hell of getting much of his stuff away.

We rapidly followed the men's example and changed into our best tunics, piled our best pyjamas, dressing-gown and a few shirts, etc., into a towel, and rushed back to the 'drome. 'Watty' was very upset, as he couldn't find any of his model petrol aero-engines, or his conjuring tricks. We left the barn with suitcases broken open and their contents strewn all over the hay.

As we drove down the road, I noticed that some of the Army were taking an interest in the barn. When we got back to the 'drome we found that most of the men had left, and the few remaining ones were waiting for our transport. They had left all the tool-kits behind, and spares, so here we were a crowd of pilots, just enough 'planes to go round, and no transport. The atmosphere was not at all cheery.

Ops 'phoned us up and started talking about doing another ground-straff. We did not think it was a good idea, and said so: ground-straffing tanks with machine-guns didn't seem to have any effect at all. We told them that no troops were visible. As far as I could see, the Panzer divisions were miles in advance of everything else, and were in no way supported. "What the hell are the Army doing? They're running away from damn all."

No sooner had I said that than the Army appeared in the doorway. "Can you do a job for us? We have lost touch and haven't got any Lysanders left. Will you go up and tell us where the line is?" – "Hell!" I answered, "there isn't a bloody line. Half the trouble with you is you seem to imagine a nice straight line with Jerries one side and us on the other. The only way we can tell if we are over enemy-occupied territory is by going damned low to see if we get shot at; and that isn't reliable, as the blasted French shoot at anything. The difference between them and the Jerry is that the French never get near you, and Jerry generally manages to hit you. Well, O.K., I'll have a shot at it, though I don't suppose I'll be able to see much."

This was when we missed the crews: instead of shouting, "Start up!" we had to do it ourselves. I sat in the cockpit while Dickie and Robbie frantically wound the handles. At last, she started, and off I went, not at all picking it.[17]

I kept low and hared off eastwards, keeping a jolly good look-out for any M.Es. It wasn't long before someone started potting at me; by the accuracy of the shooting, I guessed it to be French! 'I wish the hell they wouldn't, though: the black bursts will show anybody who is about that someone is there. I don't at all like the idea of a shower of 109s jumping on me.' Beneath me the countryside flashed by. It seemed very empty – no people, no cattle: just empty fields and empty roads.

I got to Lille, and was received with a shower of pom-pom shells from the outskirts. 'Rather Jerry-like,' I thought. I quickly turned south. 'Damn your eyes! a hole has appeared in your wing – somebody is getting accurate.' I soon reached Valenciennes, which judging by the showers flying up to meet me was definitely in Jerry hands. 'Ah, something to shoot up: a line of grey lorries.' I roared along the road, giving them a long burst. No results visible. 'No, you don't, blast you!' Out of the corner of my eye I distinctly saw the field-grey uniform of some Jerry machine-gunners. 'Right! you shoot at me; I'll shoot at you.' I swung round. A shower of pom-pom shells just missed me. 'Sights on to you; now my friends.'

A quick burst, a fleeting glimpse of men lying on the ground, then home. Well, some of those little Fritzes wouldn't get home to their mothers. 'Hell to this! If I'm not careful I shan't, either.' The ground defence shot at me all the way to Arras; as far as I could see, Arras itself was putting up quite a fight, and seemed to be still in our hands.

---

[17] "Picking it" means liking it or choosing it.

'Well, I've had enough of this; back to Merville.' I landed and told the Army boys what "gen" I knew; they seemed to have lost touch with their Army.

It was quite late in the afternoon by now, so I suggested a spot of lunch at my last night's billet. Within three minutes we were walking up the short garden path, licking our lips, thinking of a good simple lunch of eggs and bread and butter. I knocked at the door – no reply. We hammered at the door – still silence. I gave it a push, and the door opened. We went into the kitchen-cum-living-room. The table was covered with dirty dishes of a hastily taken meal; the house was absolutely empty.

It was strange: when I had left it, it was so full of life and atmosphere; now it was empty and dead. The bedroom was just as poor Banks and I had left it. We ransacked the kitchen, to find only a few stale crusts of bread: the eggs and butter had vanished, too – with the occupants, I suppose. The boys who were with me were not amused. We left the house and its untidy table without having anything to eat or drink. A gloom descended over us. Would we ever see our homes again? That wasn't a question that we asked each other; it was what we were all thinking.

Back to our 'planes. Hullo! a visitor! Wing-Commander Manston wanted to borrow a 'plane and go and have a flight. Hell! was he mad? I did my best to tell him that it was damned silly, that he might run into impossible odds if he went alone. Nothing would deter him. There was another point: we had only just enough 'planes to go round; what would happen if he didn't get back? He said, "Well, you can have my car; it's got enough petrol to get to Boulogne." – "O.K., sir; if you insist, you can have one." Off he went. Well, that's that, we thought. Don't let anyone get near that car. Poor Dick would have a tough drive if his 'plane didn't come back.

We sat about and waited, not feeling at all happy with life. Several of the Squadrons had already left for England. But we were told that we would be escorting the transport aircraft back later that evening.

We didn't like the way that the inhabitants had walked out. Nobody in authority seemed to know exactly what was happening: there wasn't any actual panicking, but the panicky feeling was affecting everybody.

Nothing happened. We sat around feeling rather lonely and very hungry. Robbie and I suddenly had the bright idea of borrowing the 'Winco's'[18] car and driving into Merville to get some sandwiches for our lunch.

It was now six o'clock, and we were all famished. The town was crowded with refugees, and we had a job squeezing our way into the bar. A charming girl about fifteen years old was behind the bar dealing with crowds of people; we barged our way in. Robbie produced a torn 100-franc note.

"Avez-vous quelque chose à manger, Mademoiselle?" – "Oui, Monsieur, un moment."

She yelled through to the back room. A terrific woman arrived, and started spitting French at us. We eventually understood that she could let us have some omelette sandwiches and beer. We said, "Tres bon." In the meantime, whilst they were being made, we would have some beer. It tasted damn good as it slid down our rather parched throats. Soon a mass of extremely thick omelette sandwiches arrived, so we piled them and a few bottles of beer in the car, and hurtled off back to the 'drome.

We arrived just as the 'Winco's' 'plane landed. The boys were overjoyed to see us. The sandwiches were damned good and cheered us up quite a lot. The 'Winco' was very browned off, as he had seen nothing. He leapt into his car and tore off, heading for Boulogne. We didn't envy him, as the roads were absolutely congested by the refugees.

We sat and waited. Still nothing happened. Now and then a few 'planes took off, turning northwards for the shores of England. David Rhodes got a raspberry from some senior officer for asking if we

---

[18] Wing Commander.

could leave for England. Back came, "Wait for orders." So, we sat and waited.

A shower of Army types arrived; they said that they had been ordered to defend the 'drome. We showed them where our ammunition was, and how to work our "sheep-dippers" – the multiple-machine-guns. These were four Browning guns which had been salvaged from a crash. They were mounted on a universal joint. Our armourers had managed to shoot down three Jerries with them. The Army were very pleased to get our ammo, as they were down to ten rounds each. We gave them about three million rounds; I hope they pumped most of them into the Jerries.

At last, Ops 'phoned: "87 will take off and escort an Ensign and two Dragons back to England. You will land at North Weald." – "Come on, boys, off we go!" We ran to each other's machines and started them up. "B" Flight were to lead us home, Johnny, our C.O., leading them. We took off, quickly followed by the transport 'plane. We left poor old J standing on its nose. I looked behind as we headed north. On the horizon there was a red glow; here and there fires burnt, with black columns of smoke rising up vertically in the still air. So, we should see England again. My heart somehow felt hollow at the idea: we were leaving France to the Huns.

We all kept low, weaving fiercely. Soon the coastline loomed on the horizon. 'Hell! What's that?' – a series of black dots in front of me. 'Oh God! We'll have to fight our way home, after all.' Cold fear gripped my heart. We soared on. 'Oh Christ! They're only balloons.' It was Calais balloon barrage. We sailed across the coast.

The sun shone warmly on us; across the Channel we could see the white cliffs of Dover. It seemed to take years off us to cross those twenty miles of water. I had enginitis badly: the whole 'plane vibrated. I realised that I hadn't got a Mae West.

At last, we reached the shores of England. We crossed the coast between Dover and Ramsgate. To our right I could see Broadstairs, where Pamela would be. We sailed on, heading for London.

The transport 'planes swung on to a different course: they were to land at Gatwick.

I was happy now. We were in England again. I looked down at the little Kentish hamlets, the green fields and woods. England looked very beautiful and fresh after France. We passed just outside the silver balloons of London, passed very nearly over my home in Finchley, then round to North Weald aerodrome. We landed in quick succession, taxied into the dispersal positions, waved and pushed into the pens by crowds of airmen. We leapt out. 87 was back in England.

It was very strange being back in an officers' mess. The blokes there plied us with beer, and were very disappointed because we were all so tired that we went to bed early.

Chapter 6

First Action Over England

England was just the same. London was hot and dusty in the flaming sun. We were all given forty-eight hours' leave. God! it was grand to sleep in my own room again. Pam came and stayed. I slept a lot, as I was very tired. We went to see a show in town. Pam and my people enjoyed it a lot; I thought that it was awful. We ate at the Troc and the Savoy. At both places I had a guilty conscience, as I thought of all the hungry refugees struggling across France. As we ate in comfort men were dying in France, ill equipped, fighting a highly mechanised army which had trained for years. That "forty-eighters"[19] should have been very happy, but it wasn't. I was feeling guilty about leaving France.

When we got back to North Weald, we were told that the Squadron was going back to its home 'drome at Debden. The old hands were very pleased. I took my car with me, as I looked forward to some parties with the boys, whom I was really only just beginning to know. We flew to Debden in time for lunch, to be told as soon as we had landed that we were to proceed to Church Fenton, where we would be equipped with tools, etc.; our men would be sent up there. They had arrived in small batches at North Weald, and seemed doomed to spend days chasing us across the country. We flew up to Church Fenton after lunch, and were welcomed on the tarmac by the station commander.

Church Fenton is a new 'drome, about twelve miles from York. It has a very modern, comfortable mess. We were shown to our

---

[19] Period of forty-eight hours' leave.

extremely pleasant single rooms. Life looked up. We had thirteen aeroplanes. Our men were turning up in twos and threes, and odd pilots arrived – some who had been back in England for leave before the Blitz, and some who had come back by boat. It was only now that I really met the chaps in the Squadron. In France I really only met my own "A" Flight boys, as whenever we went for meals, "B" Flight were at readiness, and vice versa.

The Squadron was very pleased with itself, and felt very bolshie about all the bull[20] that was flying around the station.

We didn't do much flying. The great retreat from France and the withdrawal from Dunkirk were going through their final stages while we lay about in the sun, periodically going to stores to draw new equipment, and hearing yarns from the men of how they got out. They had arrived at Boulogne all right, but found no ships to take them across, so they stayed there, and were bombed incessantly throughout the nights.

Dennis, one of our pilots, who had come home by boat, had spent one night trying to sleep on a blanket under a lorry which had been blown across the road several times by near misses. Sergeant Horsham had distinguished himself by bayoneting a Jerry parachutist in the back. The Jerry had been one of thirty who had tried to capture a hospital on a river-bank. Horsham had a rifle with no ammo, so he waited until one of the Jerries got caught in a tree, and stabbed him in the back, then ran like hell and was violently sick.

A few new pilots arrived, so we got down to training them. We were patching up our rather neglected machines.

One of them that I took up for a test let me down. I took off, selected wheels up; on came the red lights. 'O.K.' Hell! damn! the bloody thing wouldn't come out of the wheels-up position. I flew around, tugging with all my force. 'Kick the thing, you fool!' I kicked – nothing happened. 'Oh, hell!' I tugged, pulled, pushed and

---

[20] "Bull" means red tape, unnecessary paperwork, official stiffness, peace-time parade-ground attitudes generally.

kicked again; by this time my hand was just about raw. 'Right now, keep cool. Where's a pencil? Ah, now where's a map?' On the map I scribbled, "U/C[21] stuck up; will crash-land shortly." I dived low over our dispersal hut and dropped the map; it fluttered to the ground, and was picked up by one of the crews. Now all I had to do was to wait till my petrol was low, then do a belly-landing.

In the meantime, I made my hand even sorer by more tugging. Nothing would shift it. I noticed that the Ambulance was doing a small circuit of the 'drome, warming up for me. Quite a crowd was gathering to watch the crash. 'Hell to this! I'm getting thirsty. Right, let's go.' I circled lower. 'Blast it! I shan't be able to get the flaps down; that means a damned fast approach.' I made a dummy run, screaming across the 'drome, trying to gauge the position that I should turn the mags[22] off, thus stopping the engine. Round I went. 'A fast turn in; here goes. Down, down. Stick back a bit; right mags off.' Crack, crack – bits of the prop flew by the cockpit. Crunch, a terrific lurch as I got slung nearly into the windscreen.

Bump, bump, and we stopped. 'Hell! Let's get out of this quick.' I tore the safety-straps off, jumped on to the wing, then to the ground. The fire-tender reached the 'plane just as I was clear, and sprayed it with foam, just in case it went up in flames; it didn't, so I retired to tea.

Life became dull. We sat around, drove to Leeds for parties, swam in the little river. We tried our hand at night-flying, charging about dark skies, dazzled by searchlights, chasing elusive Huns who bombed Hull periodically. No success. Teddy Blake of the other Flight went to inspect a 'drome to see if it was operational to operate "Hurries" from. He inspected the 'drome, then took off; he spun off a stall turn and crashed. There wasn't much of Teddy left to put in the coffin. He had been married less than a year. It was a sad loss to the Squadron.

---

[21] Under-carriage.

[22] Magnetos.

Then came good news: another move – this time to Exeter, where we were taking over the civil Whitney Straight 'drome. "Exeter? Anybody know it?" – "Yes, it's O.K.," said Robbie. "I've got a girlfriend there."

We moved with two days' notice, this time with masses of equipment and eighteen serviceable aircraft. We were together again as a Squadron, not two harried flights working at different ends of a 'drome.

At Church Fenton the Squadron had received some decorations. Johnny, our C.O., was awarded the D.F.C. and D.S.O., David Rhodes a bar to the D.F.C., 'Dusty' Miller and 'Dimmy' Deacon the D.F.C. There was a terrific party to celebrate. We arrived at Exeter in Squadron formation, feeling in fine form. The 'drome was being enlarged – the red soil of Devon was laid bare in many places; workmen were digging and shovelling it, piling it up in huge heaps, making the 'drome visible for miles around. There was a club-house and one hangar.

We landed, and were waved to the far end of the 'drome, where we dispersed the 'planes. A lorry came and drove us to the mess, where we had a conference. There was nowhere to live on the camp; and it had been decided that we should be billeted in hotels in the town.

We piled into the lorry and tore down to the town, where we went to one of the big hotels. There arrangements were made to billet us. We had nearly a floor to ourselves, and were put two in a room. I shared a room with Chris. Robbie and Dick were together, 'Ben' and 'Watty', David and 'Mitch'. Things looked O.K. It was rather a smart hotel, with several comfortable bars. Luxury.

"Now who will be at readiness in the morning? O.K., David; I'll toss you which flight does it." David lost, so his boys would do it. Our men arrived that night: they were billeted in a big country house near the 'drome. Johnny, who was in charge of the 'drome, did some very swift work, commandeering buses, lorries and cars. He managed to get hold of a Ford V8 for me. That suited my boys fine; it carried six of us easily and would do a very wobbly ninety.

We soon settled in. The clubhouse had a small restaurant, where we had our meals; tents were put up at our dispersal points; we put beds in them and slept there when we were at early readiness. The telephone woke us at four-thirty; our engines were warmed up, we pulled our trousers over our pyjamas and retired to our beds. Sometimes enemy patrols came through at first light, then we tore off the ground, cleaving a path through the thin fog that hung over the 'drome. We chased many elusive plots of Jerry aircraft with no success. We flogged many times up to 25,000 chasing evasive smoke-trails made by the high-flying recco 'planes. We never caught them.

Action at last. Sergeant Horsham came in to land with his gun-ports gaping. "What luck?" – "I had a crack at a Heinkel over Portland; the b------ disappeared into the clouds. I can't even claim a damaged," he said.

Things began to happen. The C.O., Johnny, Dickie and Paul Grierson found twelve M.E. 110s south of Portland. Johnny knocked down two, Dickie one confirmed and one probable, and Paul one confirmed; none of our 'planes was damaged. We were all as pleased as Punch, and had a grand party at our pub that night.

At last, the thing that we had been expecting happened: Johnny was promoted to 'Winco' and posted as Station commander. 'Shuvvel' was made C.O. We all liked 'Shuvvel' a hell of a lot. Johnny still flew with us quite a lot; he was a grand Station master, as he knew exactly what we wanted. 213 Squadron arrived; they seemed a good crowd and had done quite a lot of fighting over Dunkirk. It made life much easier for us. We had nicknamed one of our new pilots 'Rubber', because he bounced.

"Come on, 'Rubber'; we're readiness at dawn, let's see a quick 'flick'." We had just been released, so we grabbed a supper and raced down the town with some of the boys in the back. "Look out, 'Widge', here's a steep turn; oh Christ! we just missed a lorry. 60, 70, 80" – prayer from the back. A scream of brakes as we arrive at the 'flick'-house. We charge in, looking very scruffy in our dark blitz shirts and oily uniforms. We laugh a lot at the 'flicks'; we hurtle out, dive for the car. "What about a spot of fish and chips?" – "O.K., old boy." We go into the rather rough little shop that sells damned good fish and chips; we sit down at bare tables. "A couple of sixpennies, please, miss." A large slab of fish and a shower of chips arrive, plus the usual huge bottle of vinegar.

A cup of coffee, and off we go to the 'drome. "Hell, and damnation!" comes from 'Rubber' as he falls over the guy-ropes. I laugh like hell, a second later splutter in the dust as I follow his bad example. Moans from the inside of the tent. Dennis, who was already asleep, wakes up cursing. We duck in under the laced-up fly-sheet. Blast it! the telephone goes for a six on the floor. At last, we have some light from a torch. We undress quickly, carefully leaving scarfs, trousers and jackets where we can get at them quickly; we climb into our beds between the rough blankets. "You swine, 'Rubber'! Where the hell did you get that from?" 'Rubber' clambers into a luxurious sleeping-bag; I think I must get one of those. A few snorts and grunts and we drop off to sleep.

Br . . . ing! br . . . ing! Hell! the 'phone. I reach out. "A" Flight here. O.K. We are at readiness now. Press the bell, 'Rubber'." The bell rings in the men's tent; they run out, and in a few moments the engines roar into life.

We clamber out of bed, shivering in the grey dawn, shove our trousers and flying-boots on, and stagger out of the tent. Weather's not too bad: no cloud, slight ground-mist – another fine day by the look of it. Back to the tent and into bed again. It's five o'clock; we get relieved for breakfast at eight-thirty.

As the light improves, we get our books out and read quietly. Br ... ing! br . . . ing! br ... ing! "'A' Flight, start up." – "Right." – "Patrol Portland."

We grab our tunics and Mae Wests; the engines splutter into life. 'Rubber' had pressed the button that set the klaxon going as soon as I had said "Start up!"

We run to our machines; within a few seconds we are screaming across the ground in a rough vic formation. I turn the R.T. on. "Hullo, Crocodile! Suncup Red 1 calling. Are you receiving?" – "Hullo, Red 1! Crocodile answering. Receiving you loud and clear." We head eastwards, climbing hard. Hell! There's a pile of cloud over the coast. We climb through it, 'Rubber' and Dennis coming in close to keep me in sight.

We get out of cloud and are dazzled by the sun. We soon reach 15,000. "Hullo, Crocodile! Angels now reached; standing by." – "Hullo, Red leader! Break away one 'plane to patrol below clouds; maintain your height." – "Hell! that means they don't know what height they're at." – "Hullo, Red 3! ('Rubber'). Break away and patrol Portland beneath cloud." 'Rubber' breaks away and disappears downwards.

The sun gets warmer; we go in big circles.

"Hullo, Red 1! Bandits approaching you from the south; height unknown." Hell! We peer southwards. Wish the Hell they would give us some height.

Suddenly, faintly, comes, "Red 3 calling! Tally-ho, tally-ho! Nine bandits approaching Portland." Hell! I waggle my wings and dive steeply. Dennis goes with me through the cloud. We come out west of Portland and hurtle flat out eastwards. It's hazy under the cloud – I can't see a thing. "Hullo, Red 3! Red 1 calling. Where are you?" No reply. Hell! We streak across Portland at 5,000 feet – nothing. "Hullo, Red 1! Crocodile calling. Bandits are on their way home. Return to base and pancake." We race for home.

'God! I wonder what's happened to 'Rubber'?' We are in sunshine before we reach the 'drome, which we see shining red in the distance, the grass wet with dew-glints in the sun. We touch down. Thank God, 'Rubber's' 'plane is at dispersal point already – I see it as I taxi in.

"Hullo, 'Rubber'! How did you get on?" – "Well, old boy, sir, I ran into nine Junkers 87. I had a good crack at one of them before they saw me; they broke up and started shooting at me, so I popped into the cloud. I came out again to see if I could find any single 'planes to shoot at, but they had all disappeared. I definitely damaged one of them, as a huge chunk of panel fell off and nearly hit me." – "Hell! 'Rubber', I wish we had been with you. We hurtled down through the clouds as soon as we heard your tally-ho. Anyway, you made the b------s turn back. They didn't drop any bombs." "Blast it, 'Widge'! why the hell weren't we there?" said Dennis.

"Christ! good show, boys. Here come Robbie's boys. Wonder what's for breakfast." – "Morning, 'Widge'. What were you after?" – "Good show, 'Rubber'! Wish I had been with you. If there's any mail for me, bring it down, old boys." – "Bring ours," said Sergeant Powell and Connoly to 'Rubber'.

"Now steady, 'Widge': we want to arrive at breakfast safely." We roar down the road, round on to the main road, then up the high-banked Devon lane that led to the aerodrome building. We screamed to a standstill outside the clubhouse. "We're at readiness again at ten. I'll meet you here, 'Rubber'. Blast! I've forgotten my shaving gear; have you got yours, Dennis?" – "Yes, you can have it after me." – We wander into the changing-room, well equipped with shower-bath and wash-hand basins. We have a quick shave – I cut myself with Dennis' darned sharp razor.

Then into the restaurant, which overlooks the 'drome, for a damned good breakfast of bacon and eggs, coffee, toast and marmalade. "What's Jane doing this morning?" (Jane is the lovely girl in the cartoon strip in the *Daily Mirror*.) "Has she any clothes on today? What are the headlines in yours? 'French fleet blown up.' God! That's a damned good show. That'll stop those goddamned Huns from getting it. Whose turn is it to have the day off?" "Chris's – he's going to Torquay. When the hell does 'Dimmy' come back from leave? He is a bastard – he's always on leave. 'Watty' goes next, doesn't he? Wish the hell I had something to read – I've finished *Gone with the Wind* at last. It's not bad; Robbie's got it now."

"Dennis, remind me to get the transport boys to fix my Standard's brakes; they are bloody awful. I'm going on forty-eighters at the week-end. I must scribble a quick letter to the girl friend. Hell! have you signed the pilots' order-book? Let's go up and sign it."

We knock at the C.O.'s door and walk in. 'Shuvvel' greets us with a smile. "Good morning, sir. Just come to sign the P.O.B. Are you coming flying with us today?" – "No, 'Widge'; I've got to wander round the camp with Johnny and site dispersal huts. They should be up in about a week, and we don't even know where to put them. As far as I can see, they're going to cover this goddamned 'drome with huts. They've even got plans for an officers' mess; that isn't due for six months yet. I suppose you heard about 'Rubber's' show this morning?" – "Good show, wasn't it, sir? We were sick as hell that we didn't see them too. Will it be O.K. if I take forty-eighters this week-end?" – "O.K., 'Widge'; that's if you'll stand by for me whilst I have a forty-eighters next Tuesday." – "O.K., sir; that's a date. I'll be driving up, if the damned car will work properly, so I can get back in a hurry if you want me. Well, we must push off to dispersal, sir; come and visit us on your tour."

We collected the mail. There was a letter from Pam, which made me very happy. 'She is looking forward to my leave.' My God! so am I.

We met 'Rubber' at the Ford, and hared out to dispersal; the whole flight was now at readiness. "B" Flight was at thirty minutes' availability[23] at the Rougemont; they had transport there, and if they were wanted, they would rush up. It was a grand morning – warm, windless, with clear blue sky. We took our coats off and lounged in the sun. 'Watty' was just finishing a model aeroplane, powered with many strands of elastic.

"Come on, Robbie; I'll shoot you for a pint of beer." We had an unofficial revolver range where we potted at bottles from about 25 yards. "Have you got any shells, 'Widge'? I've only got six. 'Watty', you owe me a dozen at least; let's have them. Where's a

---

[23] This means that they had to be able to be airborne in thirty minutes.

bottle for target? O.K., here goes. Crack, crack. Both misses. Pull your finger out, Robbie. What did you do last night? Had a bit of a party at the Clarence with some of 213 crowd; rather good types. Crack! Got it." The beer bottle splintered on the sand.

"Let's shove a penny up and have a shot at that at close range." Hell! the 'phone. "Start up; patrol Plymouth." – "How many?" – "The Flight." – "O.K."

We race to our 'planes and get off the deck in damned quick time. It's a perfect flying day, with excellent visibility. We fly westwards, climbing hard. Tiny pinpricks on the horizon show where the balloons over Plymouth are; we tear towards them. The voice on the R.T. tells us to go flat out. I push the throttle forward and glance round to see that all the boys are keeping up. Robbie has got his section in good position slightly behind and above me. Soon we are over the big breakwater at Plymouth. I note with interest that there are several destroyers and one large cruiser lying in the harbour – so that's what the Hun is after.

We level out, and throttle back; the boys weave gracefully. Minutes pass; nothing happens. I call the ground station and ask for information. They tell me to maintain position and await further orders. We cruise up and down, our eyes glued seawards. Wish the hell that something would arrive. Nothing does.

At last, after an hour, we are told to return to base and land. "Hullo, Ops! What the hell were we after?" I asked as soon as we landed. "Sorry, old boy, some plots appeared which we thought were going for Plymouth, so we shoved you up." – Oh, is that all? Thanks very much, old boy. Sorry they didn't arrive."

"What was it, 'Widge'?" – "Plots over the French coast. They failed to start, curse them! Wonder what they were. Hope they were 87s and they'll change their mind and come next shot. David will be hopping.[24] Wonder how long his boys took getting up here. 'Phone up

---

[24] Hopping means annoyed.

and ask him." – "Hullo, David! Morning, old boy. The flap was damn all. How long did it take you to get up? Fourteen minutes. Not bad, old boy. Don't be late relieving us for lunch, will you? We nearly had some fun this morning. 'Rubber' ran into nine 87s beneath the cloud when Dennis and I were above it. He had a crack at one, then ducked into the cloud. He's making no claim. See you anon. Cheerio! Oh, by the way, I'm going on forty-eighters on Saturday, so don't think that you are. What, you were? Well, I've beaten you to it, old boy. Au revoir.

"Now, Robbie, what about our shooting match?" – "O.K., 'Widge'; let's start again." We crack away, and at last finish our ammo, with Robbie the winner. We pull our beds out and lie in the sun. Conversation falls off. I lie and wonder how long this goddamned war will go on, and wonder what the world will be like afterwards. The time passes slowly. The sky is very blue – almost Mediterranean. That's just where Pam and I should be now – we had planned to spend a month on a lovely yacht cruising to Greece. What a wizard time we would be having! Instead of that we are fighting the blasted Huns. Still, the sun is shining, and only two more days to my forty-eighters. Only another hour to go to lunch.

A staff car was trundling across the 'drome – Johnny and 'Shuvvel' doing their siting. They came and chatted. I walked round the adjoining field with them, trying to decide where to put our dispersal hut. We decided on a site next door to a high Devon bank alongside a haystack. Off they drove, and I retired back to my bed in the sun.

At last, one o'clock came and – miracles are never over – "B" Flight arrive punctually. "Good show, boys!" As soon as they reach their dispersal point, we pile in the Ford and rush to the mess. It's our afternoon at thirty minutes; we come to readiness at dusk. "Anybody coming shopping in the town? 'Watty', Dennis? O.K. We'll leave at about two-thirty. We must see Ops and make up our minds where we're going and leave them the 'phone numbers."

74

"You might pick me up at the Rougers," said Robbie as we finished lunch. "I want to leave my car at a garage and get something done about the goddamned gear-box – it really won't go much farther, by the sound of it." – "O.K., Robbie, but for Heaven's sake make sure that Ops knows exactly where you are. It's a lovely day for some visitors from Germany. Come on, 'Watty'; I'll give you five minutes. What 'flick' are you seeing tonight? *Pacific Liner*? It's pretty bloody, I believe. I must just scribble a letter to my blasted insurance company otherwise my car will be off the road, too; then let's go."

We drove down, after putting our names in the book at Ops. The town was crowded with shoppers: most of us were still buying shirts and towels, etc., to replace those that we had left in France. The shops had quite a decent selection.

We left a message at the Rougers for Robbie to meet us at Fortes for tea: there was a tea dance on there, and Dennis thought he might find something worth looking at there. It was hellishly hot, so I was quite happy sitting by an open window watching the dancers, while Dennis whirled an attractive girl (but I thought her dumb) round the floor.

Oh God! why must the world have wars? Pamela and I should be in the South of France, happy in the sunshine. We were in the sun, but not together, and we were not happy, with death lingering in the shadows. Christ, what a life! Another dumb blonde was talking to Dennis. I'm fed up with this.

Thank God, Robbie is weaving his way between the packed tables towards me. "What cheer, 'Widge' old boy. How goes the shopping?" – "O.K., Robbie. I've got some fantastic pyjamas and a new dark blue blitz shirt. What news of snorting Lizzie?" – "Got to have a new gear-box, old boy. They're trying to get one from a scrap-heap; if they can't, it will cost a packet." – "When are you off on forty-eighters?" – "Tomorrow morning, God willing. Hope the hell there isn't a blitz in the meantime; my one great fear is that I'll have to bale out the night before my leave and land in the middle of Dartmoor

75

or 'the drink'. Whew! Where on earth did Dennis find that Popsie? Has she got a sister?" – "Hell, Robbie! you can have her. Let's push back to the 'drome."

The evening soon came. We wandered out to readiness, flew 'Watty's' model 'plane, managed to shoot it down with our revolvers. The sun sank below the horizon; the red Devon dust subsided as we got tired of running about.

We pulled our beds into the tent; phoned Ops several times as darkness fell. – "Can we be released?" – "No, wait for orders." At last came our release. We hurtled off to the mess for a late supper, then off down to the Rougers. We were at thirty minutes in the morning, so could stay in bed, unless anything happened.

More days of inactivity. Along the Kent coast there were many small raids; Dover was bombed almost daily. I had a long drive down to Kent for a short forty-eighters. The sun shone and, except for a few air-raid warnings, everything seemed very peaceful. The people of Kent were already used to the Luftwaffe flying over their heads; many Jerries had already been shot down in Kent.

The R.A.F. was popular with civilian England, even though the Army who had got out of Dunkirk were telling tales how they were incessantly dive-bombed, and complained that our Air Force had done nothing. They had failed to realise that our 'planes were fighting well inland against colossal odds. True the Luftwaffe had got through and bombed them heavily, but it would have been far heavier if our boys hadn't been doing their utmost. England on the whole still felt strangely confident.

Pamela and I had a grand dinner in Canterbury. The food was still very good, and there was no shortage of beer, or wine. A minor dog-fight went on over my head on the morning that I left; a few cannon-shells pattered down near the car, as though to remind me that there was work to be done. I roared across England.

When I got back, I discovered that the other Flight had been sent to operate at night from an aerodrome in the Cotswolds, and that we would relieve them after a week; then a Spitfire squadron would do it for a fortnight, so that one week per month we would be on night-flying. It didn't worry us too much; we were getting bored patrolling Portland at 20,000 and nothing happening.

Our turn to go soon came. We flew up in formation, and after a spot of trouble found the right field. It had one hut in it and a dozen tents. We soon found that it was a grand place. We were billeted in a charming old Cotswold farmhouse, owned by a simply grand old lady, who made us terrifically comfortable and at home. We soon had everyone night-trained: we patrolled over Bristol, sometimes even over South Wales. We found Cheltenham a good town for entertainment. It was grand being free in the afternoons. Mrs. Riggers, our host, lent us horses, and even came riding with us. One night the 'phone rang:

"Hullo, Ops! "A" Flight now at readiness." – "O.K., "A" Flight. Have you heard the news? Your "B" Flight boys knocked down six this afternoon – Flight-Lieut. David Rhodes is missing – two 88s and four 109s, a couple of 109s probably destroyed and another damaged." – "Damn good show!" – "O'Toole was shot down in the sea, but swam ashore undamaged. Macray force-landed with his wheels up; he's in hospital with splinters in his leg. No, he's not badly hurt." – "Hell! I'm sorry about David. O.K., Ops. Well, we're ready for anything." – "Well, boys, "B" Flight had a bit of a blitz over Portland: they knocked down six of the bastards, two probables. We lost David, who is missing. O'Toole and Mac were shot down. O'Toole's O.K., but Mac has got cannon splinters in his leg. Well, blokes, it looks as if we'll have some work to do when we get back. I damn well hope so. Poor David!"

Why the hell weren't we there to help them?

The bell rings: "Three aircraft patrol Bristol."

"Christ! Come on, boys. I'll race you off the deck, Dennis."

We taxi out towards the flare-path. On the horizon searchlights are already sweeping the sky. It's a clear, starlit night, very dark. I roar off the deck just in front of Dennis, with 'Watty' close behind him.

77

At a couple of thousand feet or so we switch out our navigation lights. I turn the compass light on, dimming it down with the rheostat. Two, four, zero – that should get me to my patrol line. I slam the hood shut, as the cold night air bit at my face; it seemed quite cosy shut in by the Perspex.[25]

I reach my patrol line and cruise up and down at 20,000. 'Oh, hell! there go the incendiaries.' A shower of sparkling dots light up the ground and splutter with a red glow. A mass of searchlights flicker across the sky. 'Blast! this is getting hot.' A series of flashes show me that our A.A. is doing its stuff.

I push my cockpit lid open and peer out into the freezing air. Below me the guns flash; here and there a red glow shows buildings on fire, explosions of heavy bombs. A voice on the R.T. tells me that there are now twenty Huns over Bristol, with more approaching from the south. Hell! why can't we see them?

I hurtle across the sky at full throttle, chasing a searchlight concentration. I reach it and dart through the beams, which light my wings with a shining silver glow. No Huns seem to be in the beam. I return to my patrol line, straining to pierce the darkness. Suddenly nearly beneath me there is a terrific explosion. 'Christ! wonder what the hell that was?' Faintly on the R.T. comes, "One bandit destroyed just south of Bristol." 'Good show! I wonder who the hell has got that?'

Up and down the patrol line for another long half-hour. At last, the voice on the R.T. gives me a course to steer to reach base and tells me to land when I get there. Soon faintly, as I get lower, I see our flare-path. I circle it, flashing my letter on my signal lamp. After a couple of circuits, a green aldis lamp replies from the end of the flare-path. I throttle back and lower the wheels, then slower still, before I put flaps down. Steady! A gentle turn, then the flare-path is straight in front.

---

[25] The hood-cover of the cockpit, made of transparent material.

A quick glance at the altimeter shows that I am still at 500. Throttle back; a bit more. The speed drops to ninety, the first flare rushes up to meet me. Hold off! I pull gently-back on the stick. Bump! Blast! That's a bad bounce. I slam the throttle open, then quickly close it. Bump! Not quite so heavy this time. Another bump and we are on the ground. The flares hurtle past my left wing-tip. I kick on the rudder to keep her straight. A spot of brake and I come to a standstill just before the red lights that are at the end of the flare-path showing that the edge is getting close.

I turn off towards the winking torch which shows me where the hut is; I taxi cautiously. Dark figures appear at my wing-tips, flashing the torch to show where I am to go, I swing her round ready for a quick take-off and switch the engine off. "Any luck, sir?" – "No, blast it!" – "Mr. Knight has knocked down an 88." – "God! That's a damn good show."

I clamber stiffly out of the cockpit, run clumsily with my parachute to the hut. I am dazzled, as I open the door, by the bright paraffin lamps. "Dennis, you old devil; bloody good show! How the hell did you do it?" – "Well, 'Widge', I saw him caught in some searchlights just in front of me, so I closed in to about a hundred yards and gave him a six-second burst. He went straight down, and there was a hell of an explosion on the deck when he hit. It was just too easy." – "Absolutely wizard show, Dennis. God, I'm pleased! Where's Robbie and Dickie? Up on patrol?"

"Hullo, Ops! How are the Jerries getting on?" – "Thanks, it was Dennis Knight who got it." – "Dennis, the Observer Corps have confirmed it for you. The Jerries are going home, no more are coming up, so I don't think we'll be up again tonight."

We sit around and chat. Dennis keeps on telling us how easy it was to shoot the Jerry down. We are very envious of him, and look forward to some more Jerries coming. The others land; Dickie in a very bad temper, as his windscreen had frozen and he had done a hell of a bumpy landing. Robbie says he has frostbite in one of his toes.

As he wasn't wearing his flying boots, we aren't surprised. We heave his shoes off and view the offending toe, which looks very white. Somebody produces some whisky and says that it is good to massage the frost-bitten object. Robbie is very disappointed, and proclaims loudly that he has a terrific thirst and that water is good enough for his toe. We all take turns in rubbing, and eventually his toe turns a greenish pink. The experts now declare that all is well and it won't drop off. Robbie replaces his footgear.

The bell rings: we are at fifteen minutes' availability, so we go to our tents and clamber between rough blankets on our camp beds. I think that I must get hold of a sleeping-bag like 'Rubber's'. We drop off to sleep.

What seems like seconds later the Flight Sergeant is shaking my toes: "You're released, sir, and breakfast is ready." I shake the others and stagger out of the tent. It is cold – a damp mist coils lazily around the tent. I stagger to the hut and sit down at our rough wooden table. There are grunts and groans as the rest of the boys arrive. We start with cornflakes and huge mugs of tea; then sausages and fried bread, bread and butter and marmalade.

We have soon finished, so we wander out and clamber into the Humber brake. The mist swirls by our mudguards as we roar down the narrow country lane. We wave good morning to an early farm labourer, down the hill towards the spire of the little village church. We park the car in the small square and run to our billets, tip-toe quietly up to our rooms, and, quickly ripping our clothes off, dive into feather beds between soft sheets. More sleep; for who knows how much work we will have to do tonight?

I woke at twelve. Robbie was singing next door. I made a rush for the bathroom; Dickie and 'Watty' were already filling it. "Come on, Dickie, get out of that bath." – "Won't be a second, 'Widge'." At last Dickie evacuates the bath. The water level sinks as Dickie emerges, for Dickie is no mean size.

We all meet in our sitting-room, looking much cleaner than when we met at dawn. "Who's coming for a quick one?" We all wander along to the Red Lion, where we sip beer and have a darts competition. The sun shines overhead from a cloudless sky. "What about a spot of tea in Cheltenham? I want to get some shaving-cream and a birthday present for the girl friend. What the hell shall I give her? Hope there's a good lunch today – I'm starved. Anybody coming along?"

We wander back to our billets. The table is laid with coloured plates borrowed from Mrs. Riggers. Our batman Jock, with his very broad accent, brings in a most appetising stew. We tuck into a damned good lunch, ending up with canned pineapple. "Well, boys, off we go." A swift drive along the straight road of the Cotswolds brings us to Cheltenham. A spot of shopping. I manage to find a most attractive and expensive flapjack for Pam's present. We roar back to the 'drome. Soon we are in the air turning our 'planes inside out doing night-flying test. We land, then streak down to the village for one quick drink before readiness.

That night we are left in peace: no Jerries cross our coast, so we loll about doing nothing. The weather is fine, so we are kept at readiness till one. I then manage to bind Ops successfully. I put it up to them that as we go back to Exeter tomorrow, we should get some sleep. They put us to fifteen minutes, so we retire to our tents. Once more I wish that I had a sleeping-bag: the rough blanket tickles my face.

Another day is past – our night-flying week has come to an end. We feel quite pleased with Dennis' JU. 88, but all wish that we had each got one.

We leave for Exeter at 11.00, flying down in close formation. We do a gentle shoot-up[26] of our billets. I see Mrs. Riggers waving from the garden. When I see the coast I tell the boys to open formation, just in case.

We land and taxi to our dispersal position. The skeleton crew greet us. "We've got a damned nice hut now, sir." We wander into a very comfortable wooden hut that has been put up during our week's

---

[26] Shoot-up, a term meaning diving low over the ground.

absence. The telephone is laid on. Good show! We give Ops a ring and tell them that we have landed. "Come to readiness as soon as you have refuelled." – "Hell's bells, Ops; don't forget we'll want some lunch some time." – "All right, "A" Flight, we won't." – "Get me "B" Flight, please." I ring up Derek Sharp, who I hear has been made the new Commander of "B" Flight in succession to David Rhodes. "Hullo, hullo, Derek! Congrats, old boy. I'm damned sorry about David. What happened?" – "Don't know, old boy. He led us into attack. There were a shower of 88s and 109s. No one saw David again. It's tough. Congratulate Dennis for his Jerry. Good show at night."

"I say, old boy, send us over your tanker. What time are we meant to be doing readiness? Oh Christ! you are a swine! Early morning readiness, boys. O.K., Derek; see you soon."

We report to Ops that we are refuelled, and sit around. The day passes slowly, interrupted by lunch and tea. 'Shuvvel' is very sick because he wasn't flying when "B" Flight had the blitz. We toss up for who should do the early morning readiness. Another day has passed.

Chapter 7

A Hundred and Twenty Plus

"Hell, it's hot! Let's send to the mess for something to drink. What would I give for a litre of freezing lager? Where's the van, orderly? Get a driver to take you to the mess and collect some grapefruit squash; a couple of bottles for me." – "I'll have a couple of bottles of ginger-beer," said 'Watty'. "Hey, Dennis! What do you want to drink? Grapefruit? O.K. Bring about a dozen bottles: Robbie will want some when he wakes up." He was sleeping gently on his camp bed in the sun.

"Hullo! What's up? "B" Flight are starting up. 'Rubber', bind Ops and ask what is happening."

Three of them roar off the deck. "Johnny is flying with them, isn't he? He's got a pile of guts; I'll swear if ever I get to 'Winco' I would never go near a 'plane again," said Dennis. "He certainly has got a packet of guts."

"Well, 'Rubber,' what are they after?" – "A single plot, sir; off Selsey Bill, sir; coming this way." – "Anything else on the board?" – "Not a thing, sir, according to Ops. You know what that means. I expect a shower of bombs will drop on us at any minute."

We sit about; nothing happens. "Hullo, Ops! how are our boys getting on?" – "They are very close together now, and should have seen it. Hold on, something has just come through on the R.T. It's a tally-ho. We'll give you a ring if anything more comes through."

"Hell, boys, "B" Flight have seen another one; they are getting all the luck."

"Hold this a second, 'Widge'; I want to give it full winds and see what happens."

I hold one of 'Watty's' models while he winds it with his drill. "Hey, steady, 'Watty'; if this damned elastic breaks, I'll just about be murdered."

'Watty' finishes winding, takes the model and launches it gently into wind; it rockets up in a steep climbing turn and starts drifting slowly down-wind. "Hell! somebody start running after it." One of the airmen starts plodding in pursuit. 'Watty', as he is at readiness, can't chase it.

At last, about half a mile away, the model comes to rest. "Two minutes – not bad," says 'Watty'. "Hullo! here come the boys – only two of them; I wonder where the other is? Good show! they have fired their guns. Wonder what they got?" – "Hullo, "B" Flight! "A" Flight here. Give us a ring as soon as you get the dope."

Robbie wakes up. "B" Flight have had a crack at something – a single recco 'plane, I think. Two of them have just landed now."

"There's the 'phone. O.K. I'll take it. Hullo, Derek! What? An 88 confirmed. Good show! What? Oh, hell! no. I suppose the rescue boats are out. Can we do a search or anything? Hell! that's tough. Rough sea, is it? Christ! I hope he gets picked up." – "What is it, 'Widge'?" – "'Dusty' Miller is down somewhere in the sea – they knocked down an 88, but the 88 hit 'Dusty' in the glycol tank. Johnny saw him going down with white smoke coming from him. The rescue boats have gone out after him and they are sending an air-search up. "B" Flight seem to be having all the luck – and bad luck."

"'Dusty' has had showers of near escapes. I expect he'll come smiling out of 'the drink'. Do you remember when his glasshouse[27] got shot off, he never turned a hair? One thing, it is a damned nice day for a bathe."

---

[27] Another name for the Perspex, transparent hood over the pilot's cockpit.

"It's just about time that we found a few Jerries to shoot at. This is really lovely weather for a blitz." – "Not enough cloud for me, old boy; I like just enough cloud to do a steep turn in if I have to," answered Robbie. "Well, here's to some shooting, drunk in grapefruit squash."

The bell rings: "Two aircraft patrol Plymouth." – "Off you go, Robbie; that's your turn." Robbie and Vines, one of our new pilots, got off in one and a half minutes dead; not bad. 'Watty' flies his model again, this time not so successfully: it takes off, climbs steeply, turns and crashes to the deck with a splintering crash. 'Watty' doesn't turn a hair. "Oh, I'll soon fix that up."

We lounge about. Robbie and Vines return after forty-five minutes; they had seen nothing. Robbie swears at Ops; they say it never came anywhere near the coast. He returns to his bed.

"It's about time somebody bought something else to read to this damned hut. Who's going shopping tomorrow?" – "We'll be able to in the morning." – "Well, boys, for God's sake let's each buy a 'Penguin'." – "'Watty', what about getting me a model 'Hurry'?" – "I can never find your god-damned shop. It's our turn to have tea first; give Ops a bind, somebody, and see if we can go. Whose turn is it? Yellow or Red?" – "Red's, I think." – "Right! Well, we'll go first. Ops say we can go now. Get our 'planes started if there's a blitz, Robbie; we'll be out like a flash."

"Pile in, boys. We'll go across the 'drome and call on "B" Flight on the way." The Ford bumps across the 'drome; Derek walks up to meet us. "Hullo! old boy. I am damned sorry about 'Dusty'. Have you heard anything yet?" – "Not a thing, old boy; it's nice and warm, but the sea looked quite rough. The worst of it is that none of us actually saw him hit 'the drink'. We saw the 88 go in – it went straight in; no survivors. We must push off to tea. See you for a drink this evening."

The mess is nearly deserted, as we are the first in for tea. We sit down, and the batman brings us toast and sandwiches. We munch them, idly turning over the pages of the latest magazines that litter the mess. All is quiet. We must rush back to dispersal to relieve Yellow section for tea.

Evening falls; the blue sky gradually turns yellow, a red glow on the horizon shows the last tip of the setting sun. We put our jackets on. 'Watty' produces his model; it flies high and smoothly, climbing and gliding in steady circles; it lands only a few yards from where it was launched. The evening is very beautiful. There is no news of 'Dusty'.

At last, the release comes through. "Come on, boys; I'm pushing straight off to the town. Who wants a lift?" We pound down the road. We meet the "B" Flight boys and 'Shuvvel', our C.O., and wander along to the pub by the cathedral and have a bit of a party. Then to bed. The "B" Flight boys go back to the 'drome and we to the Rougers. The night is very still.

Next morning (August 14th, 1940): "Buck up, 'Widge'; we'll be late." – "Hell! the damned alarm clock hasn't worked again."

I leap out of bed, wash and shave quickly, scramble into my clothes and start down the lift, still tying my tie. We have only got half an hour before we have to be at readiness: for reasons unknown, we have to be at readiness instead of thirty minutes this morning. We grab a quick breakfast and arrive at dispersal just in time. Ops tell us they are expecting a flap.[28] Both Squadrons are at readiness. "B" Flight want you, sir – I think it's the C.O."

"Morning, 'Widge'. C.O. here. Sorry you've missed your morning's shopping. I'll lead the Squadron from "B" Flight. Keep your flight about a thousand feet above us if there's a blitz, and protect our tails. We'll fix the bombers, and you fix the fighters."

"O.K., sir. What's the form? How the devil do Ops know there's going to be a blitz?"

"Heaven only knows, old boy – somehow they think there will be one."

---

[28] "A flap" means a fuss, flurry, or commotion, and so, by extension, any emergency likely to produce a fuss, flurry, or commotion.

"O.K., sir. If they come, we'll try to give them hell. I bet you a pint we knock down more than you."

"O.K., 'Widge'; that's a bet."

We sit about. Nothing happens – not even a single plot appears. Lunch-time comes and a terrific bind starts as to who should go to lunch. Ops, in their usual way, seem to imagine that we shouldn't have any lunch.

At last, 'Shuvvel' gives them a spot of his mind, and they agree that we can go one section at a time. We are told that we will be the fifth section to go, Yellow section the seventh. We shall get lunch at two-thirty if we're lucky. We sit around with rumbling tummies; breakfast seems years ago.

At last, Ops 'phone that Red section can go to lunch now. "Don't be more than twenty minutes; Yellow section can go as soon as you get back." Off we dash. The lunch is damned good; we swallow scalding coffee and burn our tongues. Dash to the Ford and charge out to dispersal. It is now two forty-five, and Robbie and his boys are very hungry. The last two sections of 213 Squadron must be starved.

We sit and wait. Yellow section takes exactly twenty-five minutes for lunch. The other Squadrons are very pleased to hear they can now go to lunch.

Once more the sun shines from a clear blue sky. There are a very few scattered cumulous clouds at about 2,000 feet. "Well, Robbie, just enough cloud to disappear into, perhaps." Everything seems hellishly quiet. Ops 'phone up, "Sorry, chaps, but you'll still have to stay at readiness; I'm afraid you'll have to have some tea at dispersal. I'll ring the mess and ask them to get some ready. Send some transport for it. I should get it across, because I don't think they have got many thermos flasks." – "O.K., Ops. Thanks for the tip." – "Well, boys, they are still expecting this blitz. Orderly, go to the mess and pick up some tea for us. Pinch as many sandwiches as you can." All is quiet once more.

The telephone rings:

"Hullo! It's for you, 'Widge'."

"Hullo, Ops! Yes. How many? Phew! Hell's bells! O.K." – "Super readiness,[29] boys; there are a hundred and twenty plus.[30] Jesus Christ! Let's go." The boys run to their 'planes and clamber into the cockpits.

"Flight, tell my crew to be ready to start up, and see that everything is set for a damned quick take-off; I'll stay by the 'phone."

I lift the receiver. "Hullo, Ops; "A" Flight now at super readiness. How are the plots?"

"They're coming now; I expect you'll be off shortly."

I replace the receiver with mixed feelings. The sun seems very warm. I look out of the window. My 'plane is only about fifty yards away. The grass looks very green now. Oh God, let us be lucky!

I sit on the bed. The hut is empty. All the men are out by the 'planes. The black telephone looks like some evil genius. Why doesn't it ring? Please, God, don't let me get wounded. Hell, let's have some music. I give the gramophone a few cranks, pick up the first record from the pile, *Little Sir Echo*. The noise rather startles me; the tune conjures up a tea-dance in Margate on my last leave. It's a damn good ballroom there, and damned good cream cakes.

Brrrrrrrrrg.

"Hullo!"

"Start up."

"Start up!" I scream.

Over the wire comes: "Patrol Portland. You are to fix the escort fighters." I slam the receiver down and run like hell.

"Start the bloody thing, you fools!"

"A's" prop is still only turning slowly over; it kicks into life just as I reach it. "B" Flight are already taxi-ing out.

"Quick, help me with my parachute."

---

[29] This means that the pilots sit waiting in the cockpits of their 'planes so that they can be airborne usually within 15 seconds.

[30] "A hundred and twenty plus" means some number larger than 120 of German aircraft.

I swing up into the cockpit. Good show! all the boys are started.

I strap my helmet on, taxi a few yards, then open up full for the take-off, just behind "B" Flight's last man. I glance behind; all the boys are screaming off the deck. I throttle back for a second. Oh, good show, boys! Dickie and Dennis are in position, tucked in close to me already.

'Shuvvel' has done a complete circuit to give me a chance to get into position. I swing in behind "B" Flight, who are in close formation, climbing hard.

"Crocodile calling Suncup leader. Are you receiving? Over." Clearly comes 'Shuvvel's' voice, "Hullo, Crocodile! Suncup leader answering. Receiving you loud and clear. Over."

"Hullo, Suncup Leader! Patrol Portland. Over."

"O.K., Crocodile. Listen out."

I glance at the altimeter. 5,000 feet. Hell! a long way to go yet. We clamber upwards. I turn on the oxygen. Dennis grins at me through his Perspex roof. Dickie the other side makes rude gestures with his hands. I give them both a thumbs-up. Behind and slightly above, Yellow section is flying in perfect formation. We are going much too fast to weave.

At 15,000 I give Dickie the two-fingers sign, that means, "Open to search formation." Dennis and Dickie swing out to about two spans; Robbie's boys follow suit. Below me "B" Flight have opened out. The long finger of Portland Bill stretches out into the sea in front of us. 'Blast! the sun is from the sea – that means they'll come out of the sun.'

Far below us I catch a glimpse of another Squadron – 213, I suppose. At last, we reach 25,000; it has taken us fifteen minutes – not bad. 'Shuvvel' has throttled back. I pull the throttle back to O boost. Dennis and Dickie weave; Robbie weaves his section behind me. I peer seawards. 'Blast the sun! Can't see a thing.'

Faintly on the R.T. comes: "Crocodile calling Suncup Leader. Bandits are just south of Portland now, heading north. Heights are from fifteen to twenty-five. Over to you – over."

"Suncup Leader answering. Your message received and understood."

We head seawards. I open my glasshouse. I'm sweating like a pig. I strain my eyes looking seawards. I wonder what Pam is doing at this moment. 'Hell! there they are.' I speak on the R.T. "Hullo, Suncup Leader. Tally-ho! Bandits just to our right. Line astern, line astern, go."

I slam my glasshouse shut. 'Christ! It's worse than a Hendon air pageant. A horde of dots are filling the sky; below us bombers flying in close formation – JU. 88s and 87s. Above them, towering tier above tier, are fighters – 110s and 109s.

The mass comes closer. 'Now steady; don't go in too soon – work round into the sun.' The bombers pass about 10,000 feet below us. I start a dive, craning my neck to see behind. A circle of 110s are just in front of us; they turn in a big circle.

Suddenly the white of the crosses on their wings jumps into shape. I kick on the rudder; my sights are just in front of one. 'Get the right deflection.' Now I press the firing-button – a terrific burst of orange flame; it seems to light the whole sky. Everything goes grey as I bank into a turn. 'Ease off a bit, you fool, or you'll spin.' I push the stick forward – white puffs flash past my cockpit. 'Blast you, rear-gunners!' I climb steeply, turning hard. Just above me there is another circle of 110s; their bellies are a pale blue, looking very clean.

'Look out! look out!' Oh God! a Hurricane just in front of me is shooting at a 110; another 110 is on its tail. Hell! it's too far for me to reach. The 110 goes vertically downwards, followed by the Hurricane. – 'Hell, you bastards!'

A stream of tracer from behind just misses my right wing. I turn hard to the left; two splashes appear in the calm sea; already it is dotted with oily patches. For a second, I get my sights on another 110. He turns and gives me an easy full deflection shot. I thumb the trigger; a puff of white smoke comes from his engine. Almost lazily he turns on to his back and starts an inverted, over the vertical, dive.

I steep turn. Down, down he goes – a white splash. At the same time two other splashes and a cloud of smoke go up from the beach. Four 'planes have hit the deck within a second.

'Keep turning,' a voice inside me warns; and sure enough a second later I spot three 110s behind and just below. 'You fools! You'll never turn inside me; turn and turn.'

About twenty 'planes are around me: black crosses seem to fill the sky. About half a mile away I can see the greenish camouflage of another Hurricane.

'Hell! where have the boys got to? Blast these rear-gunners! Oh God, my arm is getting tired.'[31]

For a fleeting second, I am on the tail of another. I give him a burst, then turn frantically as a stream of tracer goes over my head. 'Damn! We're getting out to sea.'

Below me the bombers are now heading seawards, no longer in their tight formation, but in ones and twos. 'Hell! this is too hot.' I over-bank, stick right in the bottom right-hand corner. 'Down, down.' The altimeter whirls round; 400 m.p.h. shows on the clock. I go flashing by 110s. Now I am below them I straighten out and head for the finger of Portland. The voice inside me again: 'Turn, turn.'

Rat-tat-tat, rat-tat-tat. 'Christ! 109s cannon; you silly b------!' One is past me – overshot. Sights on, I thumb my firing-button. Brrrrrrmmmmmm. A long burst from about fifty yards, a splash of oil hits my windscreen. Rat-tat-tat. 'Yank back on the stick.'

Nearly dead behind me is another 109, with two others just behind it. 'Oh God, get me out of this.' Once more I aileron. Down, down, down. The sea rushes up to meet me. I pull out and scream towards the pebbly beach about a mile away. The 109s are far above me, heading for the south. I pull up into a turning climb. The sea now

---

[31] The actual physical strain on the arm-muscles of pushing the stick hard over and holding it there in the violent manoeuvres of air combats is very considerable, for at these extreme speeds it may sometimes require all your strength to move the controls.

seems littered with odd bits of aircraft and splodges of oil. On the cliff-tops smoke rises lazily from several wrecks.

I weave gently, and throttle back. My engine has been flat out for about fifteen minutes. I glance at the instruments; the temperatures are high, but not in the danger mark. The sky seems empty. I climb to 5,000 feet. Nothing. Faintly on the R.T. comes, "All aircraft return to base and land." Thank God for that! I open the lid. The country looks very lovely beneath me. I dive. Oh God, I wonder if the boys are O.K. I dive down low.

People are standing in the streets of a tiny village; they wave to me from under the eaves of thatched Devon cottages. I wave back; I am happy – my clothes feel dripping with sweat, but I am happy. I roar along, low-flying towards the 'drome; my wings look free of bullet-holes. 'Good old A! you have knocked down seven Jerries now definitely, and probably two more.' The red earth round the 'drome looks very warm and friendly. I roar round low over the dispersal points. Already most of the 'planes are in. I turn in and do a bouncy landing, taxi quickly in to the dispersal hut.

The men leap on my wing-tips as I swing round. "How many, sir?" – Three – two confirmed, and I think I got another, though I didn't see him hit. Is everyone back?" – "Mr. Knight and Sergeant Horsham aren't back yet, sir; some of "B" Flight boys are still up, too." – "O.K., thanks."

I drop my parachute on my tail and sprint to the hut. "How did you get on, 'Widge'?" Robbie greets me. "I saw you get one of them; it was a lovely flamer." – "How many did you get, Robbie?" – "One certain; I couldn't see what happened to the rest of the sods; I am claiming three damaged." – "What about you, Dickie?" – "I got a 110 at the same time as you, 'Widge'. Then I had a hell of a time and couldn't get my sights on anything else." – "Hullo, Ops! Red Leader here. Have you any plots of any of our 'planes? Who is missing from "B" Flight? – The C.O. and Doran? Oh hell! I hope they're O.K. I am very sorry to say that I saw one of our 'Hurries' go down in flames.

I am claiming two 110s confirmed and a probable 109. Let me know as soon as you hear anything of the other boys."

"Hullo, Exchange. Get me "B" Flight, please. Hullo, Derek! How did you get on? A 110? – Good show, old boy! God, wasn't it hell? What's happened to 'Shuvvel'?"

"I saw one of my boys go in – it must be Dennis or Horsham: they are both missing at the moment. I've never seen so many 'planes in the sky before; I saw a 'Hurry' crash-land near Weymouth; the pilot should be O.K. 'Mitch' got two – an 87 and a 109; 'Bea' got a 110 confirmed and a probable. God knows where 'Shuvvel' is. He led us into a shower of 110s; that was the last I saw of him. There were some 87s just underneath us; he may have cracked at them. Ops is ringing up Warmwell to see if any of them have landed there. O.K., 'Widge', I'll let you know. Hold on a second – Ken (our Intelligence Officer) wants to talk to you." – "Hullo, 'Widge'. Ken here. How many have you got? Two confirmed and a probable? Good show! How goes our score? Eight confirmed so far and two probables? Four of our 'planes haven't turned up; when they do I expect they will have got something. I'll be over with the combat reports for you to fill in as soon as I have got these boys to finish theirs." – "O.K., Ken; see you shortly."

"Ken is coming over for all the dope. No news of 'Shuvvel'. One of our 'planes has done a belly landing near Weymouth: Derek thinks the pilot will be O.K. Phone Ops and say we're refuelled, somebody; ask them if they've any dope on our missing 'planes."

"Hullo, Ops! "A" Flight here. We are at readiness again – four 'planes only: we'll fly in two sections of two if anything happens."

"Hold on, "A" Flight. Is the Flight Commander there?"

"Here, 'Widge'; something for you."

"Hullo, Ops! Leeds here. Oh no, hell! How did it happen? Crashed in flames? Horsham all right? Where? Bridport hospital, shrapnel from a cannon shell in his bottom? O.K., thanks a lot. Let me know as soon as you hear anything else about any of the others."

"'Shuvvel' is dead. Crashed at Warmwell trying to land. He must have been wounded. Horsham has crashed in a field near Bridport; he's in Bridport hospital with shrapnel in his bottom, and bruises. He is claiming a 110 confirmed and another a probable."

Robbie breaks the silence: "Well, 'Widge', the 'plane you saw going in must have been Dennis."

"I suppose it was, Robbie. He definitely got a 110; I'll claim it for him."

A scream of brakes outside – Ken, our Intelligence Officer, walks in.

"Tea, blokes; "B" Flight have pinched their share."

"'Shuvvel' is dead, Ken."

"I know, 'Widge': Ops 'phoned and told us. Here are the combat reports. Fill the damned things in for me. There's the 'phone – hold on a second."

"Hullo! Yes. Doran. He's O.K.? Where? Portland police station? O.K., we'll send a car for him. Oh, good show! Cheerio."

"Frank Doran has baled out and landed in the middle of Portland; he got two 87s confirmed and a 109. He's sitting in the police station."

"Ken, 'phone up transport and send something for him; get on to the Adjutant; he can go with it, and visit Horsham on the way there."

"Now let's fill in these damned forms. What's our Squadron score for today now, Ken?"

"Thirteen confirmed and three probables and a shower of damaged."

"How did 213 get on?"

"Damned well. They were below you and ran into the bombers – mostly 87s with a few 88s. They claim fifteen confirmed, and have two missing. Rouge, one of their Belgians, is missing; they think he started chasing the bombers half-way across the Channel and got shot down a long way out. They don't know what has happened to their other bloke. I suppose, 'Widge', that you will be taking over the Squadron now."

"I suppose I will, Ken."

We sat round, helping each other with our combat reports. The evening gradually drew on, the sun set behind the hills; it was very peaceful. We cracked jokes and laughed a bit. At last, the night was upon us, and just as darkness fell, we were released.

"Come on, boys; I'm off to the mess for dinner – I feel starved again."

We rush up the lane in the Ford and hurtle into the mess. The bar is full of "B" Flight boys and the other Squadron.

"Have a drink, 'Widge'," Johnny yells across the bar.

"Thanks, sir; mine's a beer."

"I'm sorry you weren't with us today; you would have loved it."

"Ah, 'Widge', you must remember my exalted rank; I mustn't favour 87. I've been with the 213 boys, and managed to get a couple of 87s."

"Oh, damned good show, sir! I'm hellishly upset about 'Shuvvel'."

"I know, 'Widge'; it's rotten luck. Come up to my office in the morning and see about things."

"Right, I will, sir." – "Hullo, Frank! What the hell have you been up to?"

"Well, old boy, I managed to get a couple of 110s and a 109; then I ran out of ammo. I was surrounded by 109s. One of them eventually hit me; the engine went up in flames, so I thought it was time to get out. I baled out at twelve thousand over the sea, and got blown overland by the wind. I landed slap in the middle of Weymouth High Street, and damned nearly got run over by a bus. The police were damned good to me, and plied me with tea and whisky."

Derek said, "Good show, Frank! Where's the Adjutant got to?" – "He's pushed off home. He called on Horsham, who is really not too bad: evidently, he has got a couple of lovely black eyes and bits of cannon shell in one leg. The Adjutant says his 'plane's in a hell of a mess, and that he's damned lucky to be alive at all."

"Derek, you old devil, what are you drinking?"

"Whisky, please, old boy. It was tough today. Have you heard the Wireless? We knocked down a hundred and four today – that beats all records. We lost twenty-eight. Bloody good!"

"I suppose we must congratulate you and call you 'sir' now, 'Widge'."

"Don't be too previous, Frank. I hope so, but I don't know."

"I hope so, too."

"Thanks a lot, old boy. Let's have some more beer."

At last, after a good dinner, we pushed off to the Rougers, had a few more drinks there and got to bed. I lay between the clean sheets and thought how narrow the line between life and death was.

Next door is 'Shuvvel's' room; it seems hard to believe that we will never see his cheery smile again. And Dennis – the grand, tough, happy Dennis. 'You were such a promising fighter pilot, Dennis.'

Will I be given the Squadron? God, let me be! With such grand boys I can make a great show of it. Robbie can be O.C. "A" Flight. I think everyone will be very happy if that is so. Perhaps that is what Johnny wants to see me about in the morning. 'Shuvvel' and Dennis, may you be happy wherever you are.

Then I started thinking about the fight that day. Why the Hell did those Huns turn back? Who gave the order to turn? Was an order given, or was it sheer funk? The way the bombers were broken it looked as if funk was the more likely answer. But why? Surely, they had expected to lose 'planes, or were they so full of propaganda that they thought Germany already ruled the skies over Britain?

There were strange stories going around about captured pilots arrogantly asking for the nearest Germany army headquarters, and being really bewildered when they were told to shut up. Who can say?

If they had pressed home their attack England would have been a sorry sight. Perhaps it was true that only one out of twenty German pilots knew how to navigate; that these navigators led the formations; that when they were shot down the rest turned tail and fled. I didn't know.

My last thoughts were, 'They most certainly had a lesson today; I wonder when they'll come again.'

Chapter 8

'Shuvvel's' Funeral

Next day I woke up early. It was a grand morning. I lay in bed and thought. What would this day bring me? Perhaps the command of a fighter squadron.

"Come on, 'Widge'; get up, you lazy dog." Dickie burst in and threatened to chuck a wet sponge at me.

"Don't be so damned hearty, Dickie. We've got packets of time; don't tell me that Robbie is out of bed yet."

"Yes, he is: he's in the bath singing."

"Oh, hell! Keep me away from the bathroom, then."

I leap out of my bed. "Dickie, you swine, must you rip the bedclothes off? Anyway, at this time of the morning I'm never respectable. For God's sake leave me in peace while I shave, or I'll slit my throat. Go and get Robbie out of the bath, and tell him if he sings when we're driving up, I'll do ninety all the way; that'll fix him."

I washed quickly and jumped into my clothes. – "Come on, boys; the bus leaves in two minutes." We crowd into the lift. "Morning, 'Widge'," says Robbie as he ties his tie. There is a general fight to push the right button. After a rapid ascent to the top floor and then descent to the basement, we eventually arrive at ground level. Each buys a paper from the hall porter and crowd out to the Ford.

"Wait a moment, boys; you'll have to push, as the damned battery is flat." Curses from Dickie, Robbie and Chris, a series of terrific jerks and she starts; the boys pile in.

"Hey, wait a second, 'Widge'." 'Watty' leaps down the steps, putting his jacket on as he runs. "Come on, 'Watty'; you damned nearly missed the bus."

At last, we are off, sweeping along the main street, getting up to sixty before we are in the de-restricted area. We scream round the last corner doing just on ninety; the usual prayers go up from the back. We turn up the narrow lane, nearly exterminate a couple of cyclists and at last swing into the iron gates of the 'drome. A screaming of tyres as we stop just by the door where the notice says, "Cars must not park here," and dash into breakfast.

"What's Jane doing today? Has she any clothes on?" We peer over Dickie's shoulder; he always buys the *Daily Mirror*. Bacon and eggs arrive. We eat quickly and in silence. Our papers' headlines all proclaim of the big blitz yesterday. I suppose we all are quietly thinking of 'Shuvvel' and Dennis, who aren't with us to look at Jane and laugh with us. We don't mention that at all.

"Robbie, look after things for me: I shall be a bit late getting to readiness, as I must go and see Johnny. If anything happens, get my engine started, and I'll be out like a flash. Take the car out and send it back at once with a driver. See you anon, boys."

I get up and walk along to the offices, clamber up the stairs and walk into 'Shuvvel's' office. Sutton, the Adjutant, is already there.

"Congratulations on yesterday, sir. I'm hellishly sorry about the C.O. and Knight. I've sent off the casualty signals. The Station Adjutant has just 'phoned me and said Johnny wants to see you."

"O.K., Adj., I'll go along and see him now."

I knock at Johnny's door. "Come in."

"Good morning, sir."

"Good morning, 'Widge'. I'm very sorry you have lost 'Shuvvel'. I've talked to Group, and they agree to give you the Squadron. I think that you can cope, 'Widge'; but you must realise that if you don't, you'll go back to Flight Lieutenant."

"Thank you very much, sir; I'll do my very best."

"Good show, 'Widge'! If you want any help, just come along and see me. I'm afraid that you won't find it quite such good fun as being a Flight Commander: there's a hell of a lot of bumf work to do. Get your Adjutant to do most of the work, and just spend about a couple of hours a day in the office yourself: it shouldn't cut down your flying at all. Don't put your stripes up until it comes through from Group."

"O.K., sir; thank you very much for the chance. I shall make Robbie Flight Commander in my place."

"O.K., 'Widge'; I thought you would. Send it up to Group on the pro forma for acting rank. I'll still come and fly with you when I can."

"That's grand, sir; we love having you. Whenever you come with us you bring us luck: we always seem to find some Jerries then."

"See you anon, 'Widge'."

"Good luck."

"Thanks, sir."

Back to the office. "Well, Adj., I'm the new C.O."

"Damn good, sir; I'm very pleased. You deserve it. I'm afraid the first thing that we have got to do is to fix up 'Shuvvel's' burial. As far as I can make out, he has no relatives in England: his next of kin is his mother, who is in New Zealand. You had better write to her; and to Knight's parents. I've got the addresses and the file with the other letters written to the parents of our other casualties."

I write two letters, saying briefly what had happened and how much we missed our comrades – a most unpleasant job. Sutton was ringing up the undertakers about a coffin for 'Shuvvel'.

"Well, Adj., I think I'll push out and be at readiness."

"Could you see a charge first, sir? It's waiting in the orderly room now."

"Oh, hell! I suppose so. What is it about?"

"The Service police have run in one of our Squadron H.Q. boys for being absent without leave."

"O.K., Adj.; get the sergeant discip. to bring him in."

The Adjutant kicks the wall – the signal for the orderly corporal to come in: no bells had been put in yet.

"Bring in the charge now, sir? Very good."

"Prisoner, attention. Quick march. Right turn. Left turn. Halt. A.C. Wales, sir."

"No. 5467834 A.C.1 Wales?"

"Yes, sir."

"You are charged with whilst on active service being absent without leave from 08.00 until apprehended by Corporal Rodson of the Service Police at 16.00 hour. on the 16.8.40. Corporal Rodson, what have you to say in evidence?"

"Sir, at 16.00 hours on the 16.8.40 I was patrolling High Street when I saw this airman coming out of a cinema. I said to him, 'Airman, let me see your pass.' He said, 'I have no pass; I was fed up, so I have had a day off.' I took his name and escorted him back to the guardroom."

"Thank you, Corporal. – Well, Wales, what have you got to say?"

"I am sorry, sir; I haven't been out of camp since I have been here, sir, and I wanted to do some shopping."

"Did you ask for a pass?"

"No, sir."

"Why not?"

"I don't know, sir."

"Well, Wales, as you well know, there is a war on; you let yourself down and you let your Squadron down by being absent without permission. – May I have the man's conduct sheet, Sergeant? Thank you. – I see from your record sheet that you have only been in the Service three months, and that up to now you have got a clean sheet. Have you anything to say in your defence?"

"No, sir."

"You are confined to camp for seven days. Remember when you want to go out again, to get a pass."

"Very good, sir."

"Carry on, Sergeant."

"Prisoner, right turn. Quick march. Right turn. Left turn. Halt."

The door shuts. I have done my first job as C.O. "Well, Adj., was that O.K.? Why are some men such damned fools?"

"That was very good, sir. I hope you won't have too many to do. I'll get the discip. sergeant to see that the men get passes when they ask."

"Well, Adj., I'm off to dispersal point. Oh, by the way, get some pro formas out to promote Robbie to Acting Flight Lieutenant. I'll sign them at lunch-time."

"O.K., sir; I'll fix that and 'Shuvvel's' funeral."

I roar out and call at "B" Flight on the way. "Derek, you old bastard, I'm the new C.O."

"Damned good show, 'Widge'! That's a grand show! Hey, boys, you've got to say 'sir' to the 'Widge' now – that's right, isn't it, sir?"

"Only in working hours, boys – or, at least, when other people are listening. Well, as you can guess, I shall lead the Squadron from "A" Flight. Johnny, when he flies, will lead us with you boys. See you at lunch."

I bump across the 'drome to "A" Flight. "Congratulations, Robbie; you're the new Flight Commander. Johnny has made me C.O."

"That's grand, 'Widge'; thanks a lot for giving me the Flight. I suppose that you will still fly with us?"

"I shall, Robbie; so, you will still be Yellow leader. Your first job will be to get Squadron Leader's markings on mighty *Figaro*."[32]

"O.K., 'Widge'; I'll get it done right away." "What's the form at the moment?" "Nothing, old boy – not a plot has appeared today." "Where the hell is my Mae West? Thank you, 'Rubber'."

All was quiet for the next few days except for occasional single recco 'planes that we never caught.

---

[32] I called "A", my aircraft, *Figaro*, because I had had the little cat Figaro, of Disney's film, painted on the side panel, in the act of smashing a swastika.

The next morning at the office the Adjutant said, "The funeral is at two-thirty tomorrow. I have asked Warmwell to get a wreath for us."

"Thanks, Adj.; Derek, Dickie and I will fly over to Warmwell. For God's sake 'phone Warmwell and make dead sure that they have the wreath ready."

"Right, sir."

"I'll be in Ops if you want me, then out at "A" Flight."

I walked along to the Ops room; it was still very crude; a huge map spread on a wooden table nearly filled the room. The controller sat on a raised dais; round the table about half a dozen W.A.A.Fs. sat with headphones on. They received plots from the Observer Corps and from Group. On the table they had little notices showing what each raid consisted of and its height. These they pushed across the board. Other plotters pushed coloured plaques which represented fighters. The controller tried to get the fighters to intercept the enemy plots.

"Morning, 'Widge' – sorry, I mean sir."

"Good morning, old boy; any activity this morning?"

"Only the usual early morning recco 'plane; it came alone at 25,000 feet today. 213 chased it, but were miles underneath it. It did a grand tour of Plymouth. What can we do for you?"

"Find us some Jerries in a small quantity."

"We'll do our best about that."

"Actually, I want permission for three of us to go to Warmwell this afternoon for 'Shuvvel's' funeral. We'll fly there. It's at two-thirty."

"I'll fix it with Group to have your Red section released till four. I don't think that there is any special flap on today. They now think that the invasion is put off for a couple of weeks. Heaven knows where they get the dope from. Anyway, they don't seem very right at the moment."

The afternoon soon came. Permission came through from Group for us to go to Warmwell. We took off in close formation, but opened up to search formation, just in case. It only took fifteen minutes.

England was looking her best in the hot August sun. The world seemed too beautiful for a funeral. As soon as we had landed, we taxied to the watch office and dispersed our aircraft near the hangar. "Hell! when did they do that?" – The hangar was minus its roof and the tin sides were bulging outwards.

We walked towards the headquarters office, past several burnt-out and flattened wooden huts. "I suppose they must have dropped these the other day." We walked into the Station Adjutant's office.

"Oh, you've come for Squadron-Leader Forbes' funeral? You might take these things; they were found in his pockets."

He handed me a small white bag. I checked the contents: some letters, slightly burnt; a wallet with several pounds in; a bunch of keys and a car key on a rubber holder which was half burnt.

"O.K. You had better go along to the guardroom; the body is there. The escort and you will go on a lorry to Warmwell Parish Church, where he is to be buried. You are the only mourners; I understand his home is in New Zealand."

"Yes, that's right. Thanks for doing all the arrangements. We'll push straight back as soon as it is over. Cheerio."

We walked along the road to the guardroom. There a huge open lorry had a coffin on it draped with the Union Jack. Standing near was the firing squad, with arms reversed.

The sergeant in charge came up to me.

"Good afternoon, sir. Do you know what you have to do?"

"No, I'm afraid I don't."

"Well, sir, we all go in two lorries behind the coffin. When we arrive at the church the pall-bearers – that's four of the men – lift the coffin off the lorry, and you follow them into the graveyard. You take up your positions on the other side of the grave to the firing squad; I give the orders to fire and to sound the Last Post. When the coffin is lowered you salute, then step forward and throw some earth on it. Before you leave the graveside, you salute the head of the grave."

"O.K. Derek, Dickie. I think we've got the right idea. Have you got the wreaths?"

"Yes, sir – one from 87 Squadron and one from the Station at Exeter, and another from Warmwell. It would be best, sir, if you carried one each and put it by the head of the grave."

"Right. Well, let's start."

We clamber into the lorries and move off at funeral speed. It seems impossible to believe that the Union Jack covers the remains of the cheerful 'Shuvvel'. We crawl along the road. For God's sake, why the Hell can't we get a move on? What the Hell is the use of prolonging the agony? We pass through a narrow lane lined with oak trees. Oh, 'Shuvvel', why were you so reckless?

We come to a halt. I jump down. We are by a high stone wall; behind it is the small village church, a warm grey in the sun.

The pall-bearers lift the coffin on to their shoulders, the Union Jack nearly slips off. We follow behind the coffin, up through the wooden lych-gate, up a stone path round to the graveyard. The rows of gravestones look very neat in the thick, uncut grass. It looked all right until you saw that hole, surrounded by newly dug earth; it is in the shadow of tall trees that surround the church.

'You would love your graveyard if you could see it, "Shuvvel"; it is very peaceful. Perhaps you can see it: I wonder if you are smiling at us now.'

The Padre was in the graveyard in his flowing robes. The coffin was laid by the grave; we took up our positions opposite to the firing party; the Padre stood at the head of the grave and said the burial service: "Earth to earth, dust to dust," etc., etc.

My thoughts were elsewhere – with 'Shuvvel' at a party in Leeds. I was suddenly startled into reality by the firing squad: they fired rather a ragged volley. A few leaves dropped down from the overhanging branches of the trees. The coffin was lowered slowly into the hole; the flag had been removed. The brass plate and fittings glinted in the sun: "Richard William Forbes. Royal New Zealand Air Force."

I stooped down, picked a handful of earth and threw it on top of the coffin. "'Shuvvel', I'm sure we shall meet. Happy hunting." Derek and Dickie threw earth in the hole. It looked very deep – most unpleasant if someone fell in on top of the coffin! The Last Post rang through the air.

The service was over. I walked round to the head of the grave and saluted. "Au revoir, 'Shuvvel'; you leave behind happy memories."

We walked out of the shade of the trees into the brilliant sunshine. Back to Warmwell – faster this time – and back to Exeter by 'plane.

One day 'Watty' and I were sent after a recco 'plane reported approaching Plymouth at 15,000 feet. We just reached the outskirts of the town when, inland of us, a series of black bursts appeared.

'Hell! what on earth are they shooting at? Tally-ho, tally-ho! One bandit, over Plymouth.'

'There he is. Here goes. This is where I carry out a quarter attack. Wonder what the hell it is?' I swing round to cut him off. 'Watty' is just by me, throttle hard forward. 'What a piece of cake! One Dornier and two of us. Hey! he's going damned fast.'

Instead of closing, we seem to be getting farther away. 'Blast you! not so fast.' He has gone into a steep dive. Damn! it will be an astern attack, after all. Damn and blast! we aren't gaining.

We're across the coast now, going flat out. I switch on the reflector sight. 'He's much too far away – about a thousand yards. Blast!' I shove the throttle. 'Damn! it's hard against the stop already. Oh, Hell's bells! not so far away are clouds: if he reaches those, I'll never get him. We're down to ten thousand now, so here goes with the tit.' A jerk and my speed increases. Just behind, 'Watty' is going flat out, black smoke pouring from his exhausts.

I peer through the reflector sight. 'We're gaining slowly. About 800 yards now – still much too far. The clouds are only a few miles in front now. Hell to this! Damn! the engine's getting a bit warm.' All my temperature instruments show high readings. 'Oh damn! he has reached the first clouds.' In a flash I am enveloped in white wisps of cloud. I shove the stick forward and dive out of the bottom. I peer forward – nothing is in front. 'Hell's bells! he's got away!'

I swing round for the coast. 'Watty' appears out of the cloud just to my right. I waggle my wings, release the tit, and throttle back. 'Watty' closes formation; he shakes his fist at the clouds and makes the thumbs-down sign.

"Hullo! Crocodile! Suncup leader here. I regret to say that Bandit has got away seawards. We have given up the chase."

"Hullo! Suncup leader. Return to base and land."

"O.K., Crocodile."

We swing eastwards. We must be a hell of a long way out: there is no sign of the coast. Minutes pass that seem like hours. I fish the map out of the map-case. Damn, the coastline goes in nearer Exeter. I swing farther round to the north. At last, on the horizon looms up the shape of cliffs. We swing much more eastwards. Now I know where I am. Below stretches the harbour of Brixham. I dive lower. Yes, there it is – the little café that I used to have cream teas at when I was in hospital at Torquay. How peaceful it looks! We carry on along the coast, and at last the estuary comes into sight and the town of Exeter glinting in the sun. We land and taxi in. Jump out.

"'Watty', what a hell of a bind![33] Christ! I thought we had him cold. I was going to do a quarter attack on him when he just opened his throttles and left us standing. I was balls out with the tit pulled. We were just gaining on him when he made the clouds. What the hell was he?"

"A Dornier 215. I think he must have had special engines in. That's the one time that I wish I had a Spitfire. What a life! I should think that they'll blitz Plymouth soon; they seem to spend their time sending recco 'planes there."

Intelligence were very interested and impressed by our story. We were very annoyed to know that the Jerries had got something that

---

[33] Used as a noun in this way the word means a bore, a fag, a troublesome incident. Derivation: to bind, to discuss or argue with: hence to bore: hence 'a bind', meaning a bore.

would go as fast as our Hurricanes, even though it must have been a special recco 'plane.

Days passed slowly. There was a general invasion flap; it was expected within twenty-four hours, so we were perpetually at readiness. Awful flaps were going about defence of the station: terrifically long and complicated orders on what to do if the invasion came.

Ken was a great help; being a barrister in civil life, he managed to deal with the secret code words and general bumf[34] well. We formed a brains trust, consisting of Robbie, Derek, Ken, the Adjutant, and I. With that we managed to keep most things under control. On the station, huts were springing up like mushrooms. We all said that Jerry would wait until they were all finished, then blitz it like hell.

---

[34] Bumf means paper.

Chapter 9

A Hundred and Fifty Plus

"Morning, Ken. Is it true that Ops are expecting the invasion today?"

"I don't know, sir; I'll nip along and find out."

There had been terrific rumours floating around the camp. For the last few days, we had been at perpetual readiness. One of the enemy rumours was that there had been an invasion, but it had been wrecked by the Navy; German bodies were reported to be washed up in thousands on the coast of Kent. I didn't believe it much, because Pam would have said something about it in one of her letters.

Damn the 'phone! "Hullo! Yes, Ken, it is today? Where? O.K. Well, I'm retiring to readiness. I suppose we'll have to have a staggered lunch. Look after things, Adj.; give me a ring if anything interesting comes in. I'll slip up at lunch-time to sign any bumf. I'm just going along to Johnny's office, then out to dispersal." – "Good luck, sir." – "Thanks."

I knock. "Come in. Good morning, 'Widge'. Heard the news? Today is meant to be the great day."

"Yes, I heard from Ops, sir. I wonder where on earth they are meant to be coming. Do you think they'll try it, sir?"

"No, 'Widge', but I think there will be another big blitz today, I'm coming to fly with you."

"That's grand, sir. Will you take your old place and lead the Squadron with "B" Flight? I'll look after your tails with "A" Flight."

"O.K., 'Widge'. Tell the "B" Flight boys I'll be out in half an hour."

"O.K., sir; that will be about eleven."

I bump across the 'drome, stop at "B" Flight and tell Derek what is happening. Then bump across to "A" Flight.

"Is "A" serviceable?"

"Yes, sir, it's all O.K. Are you flying today?"

"I sincerely hope so. The invasion is meant to be starting today."

"It's a grand day for it, anyway, sir."

It was: a cloudless blue sky. The boys were lying out on their beds in their shirt-sleeves. – "Good morning, sir. Sleep well?" That was a crack from Robbie because I had overslept that morning.

"Good morning, Robbie. Very well, thank you. Have you heard the gen? Today is invasion day, and they are expecting a hell of a blitz. Johnny is going to lead us from "B" Flight. We are going to fix the escort fighters. Dickie and 'Dinkie' Powell, you will be Red section with me. Who have you got, Robbie?"

"I'll take 'Watty' and Vines."

"O.K. I bet you nothing happens at all, but still, here we are. 'Watty', have you got any models ready to fly? You make them and I'll break them."

"I've built you a special one, sir; it's a super acrobatic model." 'Watty' produces a beautifully made little model powered with many strands of elastic.

"Thank you very much, 'Watty'; do you think I'm getting fat or something?"

"No, sir, but I don't want you to break my big 'planes."

"O.K., 'Watty'; I trust that you will maintain this for me, anyway. Come on, 'Dinkie'; you hold it and I'll wind."

We wind the elastic up with a drill; steady the elevators.

"O.K. Well, here goes. Christ, what a climb!"

The model whips into the air, soars up to about 100 feet, rolls on its back, loops, then climbs in a tight circle. The elastic unwinds and the prop starts free-wheeling; it settles into a steady glide and touches down and lands on its wheels. A minute and a half. "Damn good, 'Watty'." I have a couple of hundred yards' walk to collect it.

We sit about. I lie on a bed and write letters, one to Pam, another to my mother, and yet another to the Upper Thames Sailing Club asking them about keeping my boat *Spindrift* there.

The sun is very hot. Ops 'phone and tell me that "A" Flight's job is to stop the escort fighters interfering with "B" Flight and 213 Squadron, who have been ordered to deal with the bombers. All is quiet. The usual arguments ensue on who should go to lunch first. Robbie and I toss up, and he loses. So once more Red section goes first, with lots of moans from 'Watty' and Vines (the new pilot), who swear that I must have a double-sided coin (unfortunately not true).

"Come on, Dickie; we haven't got all day. I suppose Vines will be all right." – "Oh, I think so, sir; he has done a lot of patrols now, but hasn't seen any Jerries." – "How much time has he done on 'Hurries'?" – "About fifty hours now." – "Well, that should be plenty. If he survives his first blitz, I think he'll be a good pilot. He's very steady."

We swallow our lunch and rocket out to dispersal. "Hold on a second. I must just rush upstairs and see if there is any bumf to sign. Shan't be a second. – Hullo, Adj.! Everything under control?"

"Please sign these two files, sir; then everything is under control."

"Are you ready for the invasion, Adj.? Have you got your revolver? – Good show! Well, keep the Hun out of the office while you burn the files."

"O.K., sir. I'll have a large beer for you when you are released."

"O.K., Adj.; that's a date. I must rush off now. Keep everything under control, and ring me if anything interesting comes in."

"Right; off we go."

"Have you fixed it that we get lots of tea, Dickie?"

"Yes, 'Widge', it is all fixed."

"Good!"

Back to readiness to have a siesta on our beds. All is quiet. Everything seems very peaceful. The afternoon drifts slowly by. My thoughts are far away sailing on blue seas with Pamela.

"I wonder if it will be a blitz like last time, Robbie?"

"I hope not, old boy; it was too hot for comfort."

"I should like about twenty Junker 87s to appear with no escort."

"That would just about suit me too."

"Actually, Robbie, what do you think the best way of attacking those really big formations is?"

"I don't know, 'Widge'. The only thing that I am certain of is that the 109s are miles above the 110s, ready to pounce on anything that attacks them, and the 110s in their turn pounce on anything that makes a dart at the bombers. In fact, the whole thing is damned unpleasant. We can't possibly get above those 109s – they're floating about at thirty thousand. The only thing to do is to try to get them mixed up, then nibble at the edges. Don't let's think about it, 'Widge'; I'm going to sleep. Wake me when the tea comes, before you have ganneted it all." "Happy dreams, Robbie."

We lie about. The birds fly. 'Watty' brings out his new model, gives it many winds; it soars upwards, catches a thermal up-current and nearly disappears from sight. It lands after a flight of eight minutes right the other side of the 'drome. 'Watty' sends a van to fetch it. He is very pleased.

"Come on, 'Watty'; hold my little devil." We wind it up; it soars up, does two loops, a roll off the top, then a steady glide. "It's wizard, 'Watty'. Blast! It's going to crash on the haystack." It does. We get the ladder to fetch it down. I am half-way up the ladder. Brrrrring Hell! I jump off and run for the hut. The orderly is already at the 'phone. "What is it?" "Super readiness, boys."

The boys drop their books and run to their 'planes. "Flight, see that my men have everything ready for me in the cockpit. My parachute is out there. I'll stay by the 'phone."

"Hullo, Ops. Squadron-Leader Leeds here. How many are there this time? 150 plus. Whew! Hell's bells! Try to get us off in plenty of time." "You'll be off soon."

I peer out of the window. The boys are already in the cockpits. – "Hullo, Ops! "A" Flight now at super readiness. Thanks a lot."

I sit on the bed, idly turning over the pages of one of 'Watty's' model aeroplane magazines. My mouth is dry. God! why must there be wars? I wonder if all the boys feel as frightened as I do. They at least don't know that a hundred and fifty plus is on the way. Suppose the two Squadrons from Warmwell go up with 213 Squadron and ourselves, it will be at the most forty-eight planes, probably thirty-six. How the hell can we stop them? I wonder what the Jerries feel like, flying in their huge formations. I untwist the cock on my Mae-West and give it a couple of puffs; it's working all right, anyway.

Brrrrring. Oh God, here it is! Patrol Portland. "Start Up!" I scream. "You are to fix escort fighters."

'Phone down, I run like hell, bound towards "A". The engine starts. Good boys! Dixon, the fitter, is out of the cockpit like a flash and holds my parachute ready for me to slip in. I clamber up the wing and drop in the cockpit. He puts the straps on my shoulders; I fix the safety-pin.

"Good hunting, sir."

"Thanks."

He jumps off the wing. I open the throttle and start taxiing. "B" Flight boys are roaring off the ground – three, four, five. I have picked my helmet off my reflector sight and have buckled my chin-strap just as "B" Flight's sixth 'plane is off.

Throttle open and we are off. A quick glance behind shows the others taking off in quick succession. I throttle back a bit to give Dickie and 'Dinkie' a chance to get into position. Johnny, the Station Commander, is leading us on a straight course for Portland. Hold hard, Johnny: we'll never catch you at this rate. In my mirror I can see Robbie's boys just catching us up; we are climbing hard.

"Crocodile calling Suncup leader. Are you receiving me?"

"Suncup leader answering. Loud and clear."

"Crocodile receiving Suncup loud and clear." – "Listen out."

"Crocodile calling Bearskin leader. Are you receiving?" – Faintly I hear, "Receiving you loud and clear."

I glance back at the 'drome. Twelve dots are climbing behind us. Lucky devils, 213 Squadron: they are after the bombers again. It's a glorious day. The sun beats down on us. The sea looks most inviting. Hope I don't have a bathe just yet.

At last, we are slowly catching "B" Flight up. I glance at the instrument panel. Everything looks normal: radiator temperature on the high side, nothing to worry about, as it's a hell of a hot day. It seems hard to realise that over the sea, masses of Jerry aircraft are flying, aiming to drop their bombs on the peaceful-looking countryside that lies beneath. Up, up. My two wing men are crouching forward in their cockpits, their hoods open. I slide mine open: it's too damned stuffy with it shut. My mouth feels hellishly dry; there is a strong sinking feeling in my breast. Thank God a doctor isn't listening to my heart. It's absolutely banging away.

Turn on the oxygen a bit more. We are now at 20,000. It is cooler now, so I slam the hood shut. It's a hell of a long way to fall. Once more the sun shines from the sea; its reflection off the surface makes it nearly impossible to look in that direction. Yet that direction is where the Hun is coming from. At last, 25,000 feet. We all throttle back and close up. I climb to 26,000, level out. On the R.T. rather faintly comes, "Bandits now south-west of Portland Bill." We are in perfect position to intercept them.

Below us, like a model, lies Portland harbour. A sunken ship standing in shallow waters, half submerged, looks like a microscopic model. Back with the hood. I strain my eyes peering at the blue sky. Nothing yet. Far below us another squadron is weaving; just below me "B" Flight is weaving violently. Dickie and 'Dinkie' criss-cross behind my tail. I peer forwards, heading out to sea.

"Tally-ho." 'Christ! there they are.' A weaving, darting mass of dots gradually drift towards us, looking like a cloud of midges on a summer evening. 'Hell! was I born to die today?' "Line astern, line astern, go."

Dickie and 'Dinkie' swing under my tail. The Jerries seem miles above us; lines of smaller dots show where the 109s are ready to pounce. Beneath them, about our height, circles of 110s turn, chasing each other's tails, moving as a mass slowly towards us. Far below, the bombers are in tight formation. Somehow, they look like tin soldiers.

'Steady; don't attack too soon.' Johnny and "B" Flight have dived, heading for the bombers; they have swung into line astern and now swing into echelon. The 110s continue circling. They seem to make no attempt to dive.

"Here goes."

I dive at the nearest circle of 110s.

"Christ! Look out."

A glance behind shows 109s literally falling out of the sky, on top of us. Messerschmitts. I bank into a steep turn. Now we are in a defensive circle, the 109s overshoot us and climb steeply. Now's our chance.

I straighten out and go for the closest 110. 'You silly b------!' He turns away from me. I turn the firing-button on to fire; at exactly 250 yards I give him a quick burst. White puffs are flashing past the cockpit. Another burst. Got him! A terrific burst of fire from his starboard engine, a black dot and a puff of white as the pilot's parachute opens. I bank into a steep left-hand turn and watch for a split second the burning 110 going vertically downwards. The parachutist is surrounded by 'planes, darting here and there. 'Thank God! got one of them. Now for another.'

Below me another circle of nine 110s are firing at a solitary Hurricane which is turning inside them. I shove the nose down, sights on the last one, thumb the firing-button. 'Oh, what a lovely deflection shot! Got him!' White smoke pours from one engine, more white vapour from his wings; his wings glint as he rolls on his back. Another burst. Hell, look out! A large chunk of something flashes by my wings; as I glance behind, I see tracer flash by my tail.

A 109 is just about on my tail; the stick comes back in my tummy, and everything goes away. Now an aileron turn downwards, down. 'Hell! that was a near one.'

I miss a 110 by inches – down; at 400 m.p.h. on the clock. The controls are solid. Nothing seems to be behind me. I wind gently on the trimming wheel, straighten out and start a steep climb. What seems miles above me the Jerries still whirl. I can't see any friendly 'planes at all. Hell! where am I? About ten miles off the coast. Hurrah! They're going home.

I turn for the shore, weaving fiercely. 'Hell! over to the west the bombers are haring back in twos and threes.' Two Hurricanes appear to be chasing them. I can catch them easily. 'Here goes. There's one. Looks like an 88. That will do me nicely.'

The escort fighters still seem a long way above me. I am gaining fast – about 400 yards now. 'Hell! the Hurricanes have black crosses on them – 109s; coming straight for me, head-on attack. Right, you bastards! I'll give you hell before you get me.'

Sights on, I thumb the button. A stream of tracer tears over my head. 'Blast! missed him. Now come on, number two.' He heads straight for me I yank back on the stick, kick on rudder and turn down on to the 109. 'That shook you up, didn't it?' Sights on.

Brmmmmm, brrrrrrrmmmmmm.

A streak of black comes from his engine, a stream of tracer flashes past my nose. 'God, I must get out of this.' Another aileron turn. 'Down, down, down. Pull out now, or you'll be in 'the drink'.' The coast is nearly out of sight. 'Oh God, don't let them get me.'

I screw round in the cockpit. Nothing is in sight. I scream along just above the water. I glance at the rev counter. I'm so deaf that I'm not at all sure that the motor is going. It looks all right. I hurtle past many patches of oil. At last, the cliffs loom up. I turn westwards. Several patches of fluorescence show where pilots are in the water. Motor-boats are chugging towards them. The sea is dead calm, glassy.

'I'm still alive.'

I skim past a tyre, many patches of oil. – 'Poor devil! wonder what that was off?' I wonder if all the boys are O.K. These damned Jerries don't press very hard. I bet they are feeling sore. Sidmouth looks lovely as I roar low over the coast.

'Whew! I could do with a bathe.'

People in the water look up and wave. I wave back and give them a thumbs up. 'Good old "A"! here we are at last.' I roar low over our dispersal hut. All of "B" Flight appear to be down. Round the circuit and swiftly into land.

I bump across the 'drome into the dispersal position; then men run out to meet me.

"How many, sir?" I put two fingers up. "And I damaged another."

"How many of the boys are back?"

"All but one now, sir. Sergeant Vines is still up. All of "B" Flight are down. Every pilot seems to have got at least one."

"That's grand. Have a good look for bullet-holes. I don't think there are any, but you never know."

"Did you pull the tit, sir?"

"No, not this time."

"Hullo, Ken! how are we doing?"

"Very well, sir. "B" Flight have got six confirmed and three probables. What did you get?"

"Two 110s confirmed and a 109 damaged."

"Damn good show, sir!"

"Hullo, 'Watty'! How did you get on?"

"I didn't, sir. Nine 109s seemed to think that I was their pet Hurricane; they fought me for about twenty minutes till I thought my arm would fall off. I only managed to get one burst in. I definitely hit one of the b------s, though I'm damned if I know what happened to him. Anyway, eight of the b------s still chased me. Honestly, old boy, I thought they'd get me. There was a hell of a bang once; the crew have managed to find five bullet-holes in the tail-plane. How did you get on, 'Widge'?"

"Very fine to start with. I suppose you saw my flamer? It most certainly lit the sky up. Did you see the pilot bale out? God! I bet he was petrified. 'Planes were whistling by him. If I had baled out I should have done a delayed drop. Who the hell was surrounded by 110s just after we had attacked?"

"That was me, 'Widge'," Dickie said. "I suppose it was you who butted in. Many thanks. I saw you hit somebody's glycol tank. God knows what happened to it. I got one of them – went in with a hell of a splash, then the 109s descended. I had a hell of a fight with them. They most certainly wasted a lot of ammo. For about five minutes solid tracer appeared to be just missing the windscreen. I smacked one of them in flames; after doing about a hundred steep turns, the other b------s went away."

Robbie said, "I've got one bullet through the wing-tip that hasn't done any damage at all. I say, 'Widge', where do you think Vines is? Did anybody see him after we had attacked? I think he turned to meet those first 109s. I didn't see him after that. I fired my guns at Heaven knows how many Jerries, but only saw one go for a burton; his wings fell off about 5000 feet beneath me. It gave me a hell of a shock. Did you see that one that crashed on the beach? There was a hell of an explosion when it hit. It must have been a bomber. Every time I looked down there was another patch of oil. Thank God they turned back when they did, otherwise I think we should have all been swimming about 'the drink'. My arm just about dropped off."

"I hope Vines is O.K. I'll 'phone Ops and see if they have got any dope on the crashes. – Hullo, Ops. C.O. 87 here. Have you any dope on our crashes? We are still minus Sergeant Vines. – O.K.; give me a ring as soon as you hear anything. – Ops don't know a thing. There has been a hell of a blitz all along the coast. They made a dash at London, but turned back. Already there are well over a hundred combats in Fighter Command."

"Telephone for you, sir." – "Hullo, Billie. – It's 213. – How did you get on? Hey, I said it first. Come on, Billie, what's the dope? – Ten confirmed and seven probables? Damned good! Who's missing? – Two Belgians? I'm damned sorry; I hope they'll be all right. We got nine confirmed and four probables. One missing – Sergeant Vines. Mostly fighters. No, you didn't get eighty-seven dive-bombers again? You lucky devils! We had the damned escort fighters to fix. See you in the bar."

"They are lucky devils – they had the dive-bombers again. They have lost their two Belgians. Do you remember after the last show, when Matters asked one of them how many he attacked, he answered, 'Me, I attack no one. I defence myself'."

He had shot down three. Now he was missing.

We sat around. The evening was incredibly still, the hills behind the 'drome turned purple, the sun sank. The day blitz seemed like some fantastic dream. The corn in the fields looked a glorious yellow. It was very wonderful just being alive.

'Watty' got his models out and we chased them across the 'drome. It got cooler. We retired to our hut and put our uniforms on.

"Ops, any news of anyone? – No. Hell! Well, what about getting us released?" – "O.K. Just hang on and we'll bind Group."

"Damn good show on your boys' part today. We are all very proud of you."

"Hullo! Group send their heartiest Congrats to 87, and say you are released till 05.30. Hold on a second, 'Widge'. Who's doing the early morning readiness?"

"I regret to say "A" Flight."

"O.K. See you shortly. You like lager, don't you?" "Thanks awfully; yes, please, Ops."

We pushed off to the bar. There was the usual terrific crowd and jumbled conversation. Once more the colours of the different bottles and the healthy tan of the pilots' faces seemed to be more vivid than usual. My heart seemed free. Things gradually became happily bleary as we drank each other's health.

At last, the party was over. We staggered out to the car; the air smelt delicious. A bumpy ride across the 'drome and we fell into the dispersal hut, rather unsteadily clambered into bed, after carefully folding our clothes, ready to put on over our pyjamas in the morning. "Last in bed puts the light out." There was a hell of a scurry to put our pyjamas on. Dickie was last, as usual. So, he had to blow the hurricane lamp out. Mighty curses as be bashed his legs on his camp bed as he clambered in.

All was silent. Robbie was quietly puffing at a cigarette. "Well, boys, I'm afraid that Vines has had it. I'll have to write to his people tomorrow. Thanks for a grand performance today. Happy dreams." – "Good night, 'Widge', sir. Happy dreams to you."

The hut was silent now, except for muffled conversation from the men's section behind a thin wooden partition. I turned on my side and shut my eyes. Once again death had been very near to me. 'Pray God that they don't come tomorrow; that would be too much. I must buy a sleeping-bag.' Before I slept, pictures of my sailing-boat floated before my eyes. I saw Pam laughing as I got a wave over me as we launched her. I fell asleep.

Chapter 10

Intruder

A few days later we were still chasing elusive single plots. Jerry seemed to be licking his wounds. We sat and waited.

"Come on, Red section; it's our turn to go to tea first." 'Watty', 'Dinkie' Powell and I clambered into the car. Damned awful weather sitting on the hills as usual. Wonder where the Blitz weather has gone to? "How high do you think the clouds are, 'Watty'?" – "About eight hundred feet, I should think." We rushed round the road skirting the 'drome. Shouted "87" at the guard as we tore past.

"One day, sir," 'Dickie' said, "I think we'll get some bullets in the back."

"That's all right, 'Dinkie', you'll stop it."

We bumped into the car-park and emerged. 'Watty' said, "Hullo! what are the crazy gang doing today?" I looked up. A twin-engined 'plane had just broken cloud, diving fast. "What on earth is it playing at? Christ! It's an 88."

I barely had time to get the words out when four objects detached themselves from its belly. Bombs. "Look out! They're coming straight at us." For a split second I seemed rooted to the spot. Then every nerve in my body screamed, "Run."

Christ! I ran. "Faster, faster."

Another second, then "Flat on your face, or you'll buy it! Now!" I flung myself down, absolutely flattening myself to the ground. My heart seemed to have stopped beating. The ground shook; two explosions cracked at my ear-drums. Thank God, they've missed me.

Rat, tat, tat. 'Hell, the bastard's opened up with his machine-gun.' A bullet ricocheted somewhere near me, with a high whine.

As I scrambled to my feet the roar of the 'plane's engines died in the distance. 'Hell! where the hell are 'Watty' and 'Dinkie'? Blast that oil! my hands and uniform are covered with it.' 'Watty' appears from the ground about a hundred yards to my right. "Christ! 'Watty', that was near. We'd better see what the hell they have hit – a direct hit on those tents."

We paced it out; it was about seventy yards from where we had stood when we first saw the 'plane. One of the bombs had landed in the top of a tree and exploded. Two others had landed on tents, and the fourth had failed to explode.

Several dazed Army troops were lifting up the remains of a tent. A man was sprawled out flat on his back. Another one was running in small circles shouting. "Bill has got an arm blown off." We helped try to lift the branch of a tree off another collapsed tent; someone was moving, trying to crawl from underneath it. We lifted the heavy branch and moved it away.

A man was moaning quietly, "Oh God, oh God." – "It's all right, old chap, it's all over; a doctor will be here in a minute." As we lifted the canvas aside, another body appeared in sight, lying motionless. The stink of cordite filled the air. The branches and trunks of the trees were stripped of bark. The Ambulance arrived and several of the doctors.

"'Watty', let's go to tea. There's nothing that we can do here. Hey, 'Dinkie', come on; let's have tea." We walked to the mess.

"Do you realise, sir, that we all ran in different directions?" "I do. 'Watty', those damned machine-gun bullets went close to me. I was just congratulating myself that I was still alive when the rear-gunner opened up. The poor devils of the Army bought it – about three are dead, I think, and about a dozen pretty badly damaged. If he hadn't dropped downwind, he would just about have got a direct hit on the main building. He's got a hell of a lot of cheek. I wonder how he found the 'drome."

We had a very quick tea, then rushed back to dispersal. Yellow section were extremely amused at my oily uniform. They had also seen the bombs drop, and thought that they had landed just behind the mess. They opened the sunshine roof of the car so that they could see if any other 'planes came. Nothing happened. We heard later that five Army men had died and several more were badly hurt.

Days of useless patrols followed. Then at last action came again. The order came through for "A" Flight to take off and patrol Portland.

I happened to be at readiness by the skin of my teeth. I grabbed a Mae West and was off the deck just in front of Robbie. It was a fine day – no low cloud, but some speckled high stuff. We climbed up, Robbie with his section the usual 1000 feet above our tails. The sea looked very blue.

When I arrived over the Bill, a small tramp-steamer was plugging slowly through the water. The sunken ship still lay half submerged in the harbour. We flew up and down, the wing 'planes weaving. After some minutes, over the R.T. came: "Bandits close to you now."

I strain my eyes seawards. Nothing. 'Christ!' Below the little ship is suddenly surrounded by columns of water. 'Bombs. Hell! they're damned accurate. Where the hell are they?' I peer around. Nothing.

The little ship is absolutely surrounded with boiling water. 'Quick, you fool! they must be dive-bombers.' I shove the stick forward, nose down, straight for the ship. There they are. A line of twin-engined 'planes are just making another run at the ship. Jaguar bombers. 'Hell! I am going too fast – four hundred on the clock. Whew! 109s!' I flash past a couple of them coming in the other direction. 'Now, you bastards! Damn! they have seen me.' The Jaguars have turned, and are heading straight out to sea. 'Steady; those 109s are somewhere behind you!' I steep-turn round the ship. She looks all right, and is still travelling through the water. Dirty marks in the water behind her show where the bombs have burst. They were all close, but not close enough.

Damn! the 110s are now some way out; about 500 feet above me a ragged bunch of 109s are heading seawards. I climb, but haven't a hope in hell of catching them. 'Oh, good show!' Plummeting down, black smoke trailing behind, in a vertical dive, came a 110. At about 5000 feet a puff of white shows where one of the crew had baled out. The 'plane hits the sea with a terrific column of spray. All the Jerries have disappeared over the horizon. I turn for home.

'Where the hell are the other boys?' I dive low over the ship. Several figures on the bridge wave to me. 'I salute you, Merchant Navy. Good luck.'

On the R.T. comes the order to return to base and land. 'Hell! I have forgotten to give Tally-ho. It doesn't matter.'

I fly leisurely back to the 'drome. 'Those boys on that ship must have been very frightened. Thank God, they didn't hit it. Who on earth hit that 110? I shall soon know.' I landed quickly just behind 'B', Robbie's 'plane.

"Any luck, sir?"

"No. Did any of the others get anything?" "Mr. Chivers is the only one who has fired his guns, sir."

"Oh, damn! We saw quite a few, but couldn't get into firing positions."

"Well, boys, that was a cock-up. It took me a hell of a time to realise that they were dive-bombing."

"You just disappeared, 'Widge'. I was looking the other way when you dived. I had just looked away for a second; when I looked back you weren't there. It struck me that they must be dive-bombers," Dickie said.

"Robbie, you old devil, where the hell did you find it?" "Well, 'Widge', they damned nearly jumped us – about six 110s. I saw them just as you dived; climbed up underneath their bellies; they never saw me coming. I got my sights on the arse-end one and gave him a burst. A cloud of oil hit me in the windscreen. I caught a fleeting glimpse of him going vertically downwards, then the others were after me. Luckily the wispy cloud was just under me, so I disappeared in it."

"I'm awfully sorry, sir," said 'Rubber'. "I saw the C.O. dive, so went down after him. Grantham followed. I passed some 109s, but was going such a lick I couldn't get round to them."

"Robbie, old boy, your Jerry most certainly hit the deck. I saw it go in. Somebody baled out of it, too. He must be in 'the drink' about twenty miles out. We had better get the rescue service out after him. Damned good shooting. I am hellishly sorry we weren't all together to help you. I was going so damned fast when I got down to the Jaguars that I couldn't do a thing; I whistled past some 109s on the way down, and was windy that they would get on my tail. So, I did as quick a turn as possible round the ship. By that time the bombers were above us. So, I didn't do a damned thing, except just about break my ear-drums in that dive."

"Still the little boat sails on. God! those boys on ships have got guts."

"A" Flight's turn came to go to Gloucestershire. I stayed behind, after promising to come up and fly with them soon. There was a certain amount of office work to do, and I had hopes of having some more day-fighting.

The invasion panic was still in the air. No Jerries turned up. Group was keen on us getting as much night-flying as possible. The boys were keen on action, and worried me to arrange offensive patrols to blitz some of the 'dromes in the north of France. Group took these suggestions well, and promised to lay it on when the moon rose. I joined the "A" Flight boys, and we were kept fairly busy for a couple of days chasing searchlight beams and looking for Jerries flying over Bristol.

The moon rose. One afternoon Group 'phoned me and said that two aircraft were to carry out an offensive patrol and ground-straff. They were to be at -----, one of the 'dromes on the coast, by 18.00 hours, where further instructions and maps would be forthcoming. I said they would be there.

"Robbie, I want to talk to you a second. Tonight, there's a special job to do. A blitz of an aerodrome on the other side. Would you like to come?"

"Rather, 'Widge'. What's the form?"

"We are to be at ----- by six this evening. We'll get all the dope from the intelligence officer there. We must get flares put in the 'planes, carry revolvers and port flares, just in case we do have to land the other side. If you do, put a couple of bullets in the petrol tank, then shove a port fire in it. That should make a 'plane burn O.K."

"That's grand, 'Widge'. What time shall we leave?" – "About five fifteen. Fix it up that the 'planes are absolutely O.K. Tell 'Watty' that he will be in charge in your absence. We'll be landing back at ----- after the show and staying the night there. – Blast! I'm wanted on the 'phone." – "Hullo! Yes, Ops. Two reserves from "B" Flight. O.K.; we'll meet them there at six. Cheerio."

"Ops say that Group have ordered two of "B" Flight to come as reserve. They might go across when we get back." – "I wonder where on earth we are going. It's a hell of a way over the sea." – "Come down and have a swift tea. We'll tell Mrs. Riggers that we'll be out tonight. Hope the weather stays fine."

We hurtle down to the lovely Cotswold village; there is something gloriously soothing about houses built with the Cotswold stone. I felt the old sinking feeling at the thought of action again. At the least it means a 100 miles of sea out and back. I wonder what their ground defence will be like. Still, it's no damned good worrying.

We have a grand tea – lots of toast, and some of our hostess' home-made jam. Then up to the 'drome.

The 'planes are all set. 'Watty', Dickie and the boys wish us good luck, and beg that they may go next time. I clamber into my mighty 'A'. Then off. The visibility is extremely good: within a few minutes of taking off I could see the sea glinting silver in the sun, the coastline from the Isle of Wight to Plymouth. It was a marvellous day.

We landed, and were met by the intelligence officer, who had maps for us. Our destination was Caen, an aerodrome east of Cherbourg Peninsula. One hundred and thirty-five miles – a hundred and thirty of those across the sea. Two sixty miles there and back. Whew! hell of a long swim if anything went wrong.

"Come on, Robbie; let's have a darned good look, and work out the courses now. Then there won't be a flap when we are starting."

"I've got a photo of the 'drome to show you, if you don't mind coming to see it in my office; it's just along the passage," said the intelligence officer.

"O.K. We'll come and have a good look now. Hang on a second; here come the "B" Flight boys."

Two 'Hurribirds' scream across the 'drome, just skimming the grass, and break away into a Prince of Wales feathers.[35] – "Damn him! I know who that is. Derek, the bastard! And at a guess I should say young 'Bea' is with him." They swing into land. Sure enough, the blue nose on the leader's 'plane tells me that I'm right; and 'Bea' does step out of the second 'plane.

"Derek, you old devil, what the hell do you mean by beating the 'drome up?" – "Hullo, 'Widge' – sir I mean – I didn't know you had arrived yet. What's the dope?"

"A hundred and thirty miles of sea to a 'drome called Caen." "Good Lord! believe it or not, but I stayed a night there once six months ago. I know it well. It's a bloody great 'drome with some large hangars," Derek said.

"Good show, Derek! Come and have a look at the photos the recco boys have taken."

We walk along to the office. It is filled with models of friendly and enemy 'planes, some hanging from wires in the ceiling, others on stands with batteries and little bulbs that show you where the arcs of fire of the guns are. On the walls hang maps of every sector of Europe.

The intelligence officer unrolled a huge mosaic photograph – a beautiful piece of work showing every detail. We crowd round and

---

[35] Prince of Wales feathers: three 'planes break formation upwards, the two wing 'planes splitting outwards, thus forming the Prince of Wales feathers.

peer at it. "There's the 'drome; it's six miles from the coast. You can easily recognise it from the railway running parallel to the coast on the southern boundary. You should also be able to see that triangle of roads just west of the 'drome. As you can see, it is an extremely large 'drome; as far as we know, there are dispersal points all round it. The hangars are on the south-east side. Those huts are only wooden; they are worth having a few shots in them. This photo was taken about two months ago, so there may be more huts. If you look carefully, you can see gun-pits – there, there, and there. They are probably pom-poms, like our Bofor guns. I'm afraid we don't know much about their defence at the moment. You should be able to tell us a lot about that when you get back, so try to remember where the gun-posts are. According to our latest information, there is no heavy flak.

"The object of this raid is to destroy aircraft landing there or parked on the 'drome. They use that 'drome for their returning bombers. You should find something to pot at.

"I think that is all I can tell you, sir. Here are some escaping kits. Group orders are that you are to take off at midnight, unless they give any orders to the contrary. Now I'll take you along to the mess."

The mess was only a wooden hut, actually quite well fitted out inside, an ante-room, dining-room and a games-room. They gave us a good dinner. We all drank orange squash, much to Robbie's disgust. I was strict about that, as we had a long time to wait, and it's so damned easy to drink quietly away, not noticing how many beers you have; by the time midnight came we would have been in no condition for a ground-straff. So orange squash it was.

After dinner we wandered into the games-room. "Come on, 'Widge'; let's take the others on at snooker," Derek said. – "O.K. Come on, 'Bea' and Robbie; we'll smash you." Then started one of the worst billiard games ever played.

None of us could hit a thing. We were very cheery, but just couldn't play. It was surprising to me that we didn't tear the cloth. We didn't, but neither did we finish the game. We chucked it up after a time, and retired to the ante-room, where we pored over magazines. When we got tired of them, we burgled the cupboard that held the library books; with the help of 'Bea's' knife and a certain amount of strength, the lock was removed. We removed quite a few books, mostly detective novels, and lay about on the couches and read.

At last, eleven o'clock came. "Come on, boys; what about going out to the Watch office and getting the engines warmed up and everything taped?" We walked out. It was a starlit night with a huge yellow moon. It seemed nearly as light as day, and was quite warm. We walked to the Watch office and warmed up our engines. My port flares were loose in one of the little pockets on my escape panel. The red lights of the cockpit seemed to give me cheery confidence.

We met in the Watch office, 'phoned up the Met office and worked out our course. At last, everything was fixed. I 'phoned Ops and checked that we were still to go at midnight. They told me to have the aircraft airborne by midnight. R.T. silence to be maintained on the outward journey. Can be used for homing on the way back. Another half-hour to go.

We sat around kicking our heels, each collecting his parachute and quietly studying the map of the target. It should be very easy to find. Thirty minutes' flying at economical speed. That should give us a safe twenty minutes over there.

"Robbie, we'll get over the 'drome at twelve thousand, then throttle back and glide down. Start your beat up on the south side. I'll look after the northern half."

"O.K., 'Widge'. If they have got any searchlights, I'll shoot them out if they get on you, and you shoot them out if they get on me.

"Right. Now don't stay longer than twenty minutes. On the way home give me a call on the R.T. You know the form if you are going in 'the drink'. Scream on the R.T. and keep calling, to give the ground station a chance to get a fix on you."

"Right, old boy."

The telephone rang, and made me, at any rate, jump. "It's for you, sir." – "Hullo! Met. Right. Hold on a second and I'll get a pencil. O.K. Now let's have it. Thanks, Met; that's fine."

"Well, boys, the weather looks O.K. I'm not too keen on the sound of the weather later on here. If it duffs up,[36] Derek, give us a shower of Verey lights to show us the way to come home." – "I'll keep a damned good eye on it." – "Blast it! I hope it doesn't pack in before we go. What's the time?"

"Twenty to twelve."

"Let's go out at quarter to and start up at ten to. I'm going to run my engine up damn well first, and make sure that it's O.K."

"I'll get mine started, too," 'Bea' said. "Just in case one of your machines is duff."[37]

"O.K., 'Bea'; thanks a lot. Where the hell are my gloves? Blast! I've left my torch behind. Lend me one, somebody. – Thanks, Derek; I'll give it you as soon as I land. Well, I think we'll wander out."

We stepped out into the night. What a night! Much more fitting for romance. Still, it couldn't be more perfect for our job.

"Well, good luck, Robbie."

"Good luck, 'Widge'; don't forget to call me on the way home."

"I won't."

"Good luck, sir," 'Bea' yells as he trots to his machine.

"Good hunting, 'Widge'. Give them hell. Wish I was coming with you now; this waiting browns me off."

"Thanks, Derek. We'll go together next time, I hope. Don't forget the firework display."

"I won't; see you in about an hour thirty after take-off. Cheerio."

I clambered into the mighty 'A', turned on the cockpit lights, and strapped myself in with the help of one of the men.

"O.K. I'll start up now."

---

[36] "Duffs up" means becomes thick with either low cloud or ground haze.

[37] And, by extension, anything which goes wrong.

The engines started at once. I glanced across to Robbie's machine – his engine started O.K., too. On with the compass light. I set the course on.

Put gloves on; check position of revolver and port-flares. Give a short puff into the tube of Mae West, just to make sure it is O.K. I feel it swell. That's O.K. The engine temperatures slowly crawl up their gauges. I open the throttle full. Revs O.K. Test the mags. Slight drop. That's O.K. I throttle back. Turn on the reflector sight and turn it down to dim. That should be O.K. I look across and see Robbie silhouetted in his cockpit. It is five to twelve.

I give him the thumbs-up sign. He returns it. O.K. Slowly I taxi out. As I do so I glance at the stars. The aeroplanes dispersed round the 'drome show up shining silver in the moonlight. If there is anything to see, we should most certainly see it tonight.

I taxi to the end of the flare-path. The aerodrome control pilot gives a green light with his aldis lamp. I glance at the dashboard clock: it is two minutes to the hour. Throttle open, I take off. As soon as 500 feet is reached, I throttle back to the most economical revs and boost. A gentle left-hand turn gets me on my course. Robbie has swung into formation on my left. We switch our navigation lights off.

The coast was a lovely sight, the calm sea reflecting the moon. Every little boat was visible. We climbed slowly upwards. The coast had receded out of sight behind us by the time we were at 12,000. It was incredibly lovely looking at the silver sea. After a glance at the instruments, I turned all the cockpit lights out except the compass light.

We levelled out at 12,000, and throttled even farther back. The less petrol we used the better. I glanced at the clock: we had been airborne ten minutes. Another ten minutes and we should see Cherbourg to our right. I have picked out a star to steer by – it is easy to keep a steady course. For a second, I flicked the lights on to have a look at the temperatures. They were slightly below normal, so I closed the radiator. I must remember to open it before I start the straff, or go flat out.

INTRUDER

The minutes crawl by. I peer out to the right. It's about time Cherbourg Peninsula loomed up. A glance at the clock tells me we left the ground twenty minutes ago; that means we have been on course eighteen minutes. At last! There it is, clear as daylight. I get the map out. Yes, there's Point de Barfleur. We seem to be just about in the right place. On, on. Only another ten minutes and we'll be there. Those ten minutes seemed like hours.

At last, I could see the coastline dead in front of us. Lights on again, to have a good look at the instruments. Everything looks O.K. 'God! how awful it would be if it wasn't. What the hell should I do? Turn back or go on and force-lob[38] in France? Don't be a fool! Everything is O.K.: cross your bridges when you come to them.'

The coast looms closer. I get my map out. 'Throttle back a bit and lose height. Good show! There's the little river just to our left. That's damn good! We are about a mile too far to the west.' I swing slightly eastwards. There's the little harbour of Landiers. (I had originally planned to fly up the river to the village of Caen; I changed my mind because it was so clear.) We cut the corner slowly, losing height. Ten thousand feet now. There it is. The town glints in the moonlight. I can distinctly see the large market square, and the church spire. It looks exactly like a toy town. There isn't a trace of light. The small docks show up as a silver oblong. There is a little steamer lying in them. There's the road to the south.

'Christ! there it is' – the 'drome with a square wood at one corner. It looks a terrific light patch: just like its photo that we had seen on the mosaic map. To the east a white beacon is blinking the letter B. I throttle back even more. The 'drome, like the town, is completely without lights.

Six thousand feet now. Nothing happens. The hangars stand up well; we are still too high to see any aircraft. The huts show up well now. There are about double the number that there had been on the

---

[38] Make a forced landing.

131

photo. Two thousand feet. There they are. A neat row of twin-engined 'planes; another row. What are they? Junkers 88s. 'Hell! and 215s.' I waggle my wings – the sign for Robbie to break away.

At 1,000 feet I shove the throttle full open. That line of about nine will do me nicely. A steep right-hand turn. Now down. Sights on. Steady. I thumb the firing-button. A stream of fire pours from my wings; back on the stick, the line of aircraft flash through my sights. 'Hell! pom poms.' A string of fiery ping-pong balls tear by my wings; another stream; then another.

'Oh, Hell! searchlights.' Four blue searchlights leap out of the shadows. 'Blast! they've got me.'

My wings are suddenly shining a brilliant silver. 'Head in cockpit, quick!' I yank back on the stick. 'Steady. Robbie, pull your finger out and shoot them off me. Thank God I'm clear of them now.' – 'Christ!' a glance behind shows me a stream of pom-pom shells seemingly appearing from a circle round the 'drome, all meeting in an apex. 'Oh God!' For a fleeting second, I catch a glimpse of a 'Hurribird' caught in the searchlights surrounded by snacky iridescent shells. 'You bastards!'

I pull up into a steep left-hand turn. 'Look out! you'll be coming out of the moon. Oh, blast the moon! Here goes.' I come in low. 'There they are.' Another line of aircraft.

Brrrrrmmmm, brrrmmmmmmmm.

'Damn those searchlights!' One is shining from straight in front of me. I fly straight at it.

Brrrrrmmmmm, brrrrrrrm.

'Got you!' For a second there is a red glow, then the searchlight goes out. 'Christ, I'm surrounded by pom-pom shells; they're all meeting at a point just behind my tail. Oh God! this is too hot. There goes Robbie.' A stream of pompoms shows me where Robbie is. Three searchlights are trying to get him. 'You b-------, I'll get you. – Hullo, got one.' As I turn left, I see a 'plane burning furiously. From just under my nose a series of flashes shower out the burning ping-pong pom-bells – a gun-post, shooting the other way.

'Sights on. Brrrrrrmmmmmm. That'll teach you. Now for another searchlight.'

I scream past the hangars, about the height of their roofs, at a searchlight that is shining at Robbie somewhere on my left side. Brrrrmmmmmm. The light goes out. 'Hell! that was a near one.'

A snaky line of shells just miss my nose. They are so bright they dazzle me. 'Oh God! this is too hot. I can't see a thing. Blast you! A gun-post is dead in front of me, its shells bursting just over my head. I thumb the button again. Brrrrrrmmmmmmmmm. Hell! you bloody fool, you nearly hit that.'

Out of the corner of my eye I caught a glimpse of men lying on the ground. 'God! that's burning.' The 'planes near the fire are lit up by the flames. 'One more dive and I've had enough. Christ, those pom-poms are hell. Brmrnmmm, hisssssshisssssss. Blast! out of ammo. Home, and don't spare the horses.'

I roar over Caen, just missing the church spire. 'You b-------s!' From the street corners and the windows of houses little flickers of light flash. Rifle and revolver fire. Back with the stick. I zoom up to 2,000 feet. 'Christ! there goes Robbie.' A shower of pom-pom shells snake across the 'drome behind me. No searchlights are on now, and not so many guns are firing. Cockpit lights on. Christ! radiator temperature 120; oil pressure O.K. Oil temperature 75, Keep cool! That's all right. It's not up to the emergency temperature.

Throttle back, you fool! before the engine does blow up. I pulled the throttle back and shoved her in weak mixture. 'Now petrol. Port tank ten gallons, starboard slightly less than ten. That's not too bad. Gravity tank full. Phew! it's hot. My clothes are dripping with sweat.'

I crossed the French coast, climbing slowly, steadied up on my homeward course. 'Keep that star just on the edge of the windscreen and that will be O.K. Thank God I'm still alive. What's the time? Twelve forty-seven. Christ, is that all? Now call Robbie on the R.T.' – "Hullo, Robbie! 'Widge' calling. Are you O.K.? Over." – Nothing. I wait a minute. Except for the crackle of atmospherics not a sound comes through the R.T. – "Hullo, Robbie! Hullo, Yellow 1! Are you O.K.? Over." – Nothing. 'Oh, please God, what has happened to him? How can I explain it to his girl friend? Perhaps he has force-landed and is all right.' – "Hullo, Robbie! are you receiving? Over." Still nothing.

The engines seem to be running rough, the temperatures are lower now. 'Perhaps I've got a bullet in the radiator. Oh God, don't let me drop in the sea. What shall I tell the boys about Robbie? Oh, why did we ever start on this show? Don't be a fool! Robbie may be perfectly O.K., except his radio has packed. But it was all right when he tested it. God, where are you, Robbie?'

I glance at the clock. One o'clock: halfway. 'If I fall in 'the drink' now I haven't a hope of being picked up. I'll shoot myself before we hit. – No, don't be a fool; while there's life there's hope. I can't stand floating about; if I drop in I'll shoot myself.'

Another ten minutes. I peer through the windscreen. 'Hell! clouds below me. Stay up above them: if your engine cuts, you'll need every foot of height.' Beneath me there was about 7/10s[39] cloud. Another five minutes. 'Except for this blasted cloud, I could very likely see the coast. It's wonderful to be alive.'

Ten past one. Time to go beneath the cloud. 'Turn on to gravity: the wing-tanks are just about empty.' I throttle back and glide down. The tops of the clouds look like snowy mountains shining in the moon. Soon I was enveloped in the white misty clouds. Thank God they weren't thick. I came out of them at 2,000. 'Thank God. there's the coast. Now where the hell am I?'

I cross the coast. 'Good old England! God, how pleased I am to see you! There's the beacon. Oh, good old Derek!' A green Verey light soars up. 'There's the 'drome.' I turn on the navigation lights and roar around the 'drome; the green aldis lamp winks at me from the flare-path. 'Wheels down, flaps down, into land. Bump, bump.'

---

[39] Means the sky was a little over half obscured by clouds.

I had arrived. I turned off quick and taxied to the Watch hut. It was pretty dark under the clouds. A flashing torch showed me where to turn round. I swung into position and switched the engine off.

Dark figures jump up on to my wing.

"How did you get on, 'Widge'?"

"O.K., Derek. Is Robbie back yet?"

"No."

"I called him up on the way home, as we had arranged, and didn't get a reply. There were a shower of 'planes. We left one of them burning. I know I hit several others. The reception was bloody hot: about twenty pom-poms and four searchlights – blue devils that were damned accurate. I saw Robbie caught in them for a second, absolutely surrounded by shells. Here's your torch, Derek. Let's have a look round for bullet-holes. It's about time Robbie was back."

We flashed the torch all over the 'plane. There appeared to be no holes.

"Did you find it easily, 'Widge'? What were the 'planes on the deck?" 'Bea' asked.

"It was a piece of cake[40] finding the 'drome. The course was damned good: we arrived the other side about a mile too far west. The 'planes were 88s, 109s, and I think some Dornier 215s: parked in beautiful straight lines. Christ! I wish Robbie would hurry up. Sshhhh! do you hear an engine?"

We stood still and listened.

"It sounds like a 'Hurribird'; let's sling up a Verey light."

"O.K., 'Widge', I've got it here," said Derek.

Crack! A green light soars up.

"There he is; thank God for that!"

Navigation lights appear, circle the 'drome; the aldis lamp on the flare-path flashes a green at it. The downward recognition light goes on. Then the 'plane turns and comes into land.

---

[40] "A piece of cake" means anything easy.

"Thank God, Derek! I really was worried: I thought he had been hit by the flak."

We ran out, flashing the torch, signalling him in. As soon as he swung round, I jumped up on the wing. There was Robbie, looking rosier than usual, his face lit by the red cockpit lights.

"Good show, Robbie – bloody good show! I thought you were in 'the drink' or somewhere."

"'Widge', you old bastard! God! I'm pleased to see you. Christ! that was a hell of a journey home. My R.T. packed up, so I couldn't call you. What a reception! Blasted accurate searchlights. I didn't know there were so many pom-poms in the world."

He clambered out.

"I say, 'Widge', weren't those 'planes beautifully parked – just right for use. Did you hit the flamer, or did I?"

"I'm damned if I know. I hit about three of them really well. I didn't see the fire break out. It was burning furiously when I looked round after my second attack. God! it's good to be in England again. Those pom-pom shells have put ten years on to my life. I could see exactly where you were by the shower of shells whistling up. I fixed two of the searchlights when they were shining at you, and then went round shooting at the gun-posts that were shooting at you."

Robbie said. "So did I, 'Widge'. I shook myself once: I was so damned low I just about hit a gun parapet. Did you see all the bastards shooting from the town when you left?"

"Yes, there were pinpricks of light from everywhere. I'll swear the Jerries were leaning out of all the lavatory windows shooting at me. That journey home! My engine felt as if it was going to stop any second. I've worn my finger out pressing the petrol gauge-switch. Derek, old boy, I'm afraid you've had it for tonight. It's damned thick now. The clouds are getting thicker, too."

"Yes, Derek; sorry about that. But it's not worth going in bad weather. You go first next time."

"Blast it, 'Widge', it's O.K. over the other side." – "No, old boy, call it a day. I must 'phone Ops. I had a simply bloody journey home, Robbie; you can imagine what I felt like when you didn't answer on the R.T."

"Ops want you to ring them, sir," said the duty pilot as soon as we got inside the hut.

"Hullo, Ops! C.O. 87 here. May I speak to the controller? Hullo, sir! Leeds here. We found it O.K., sir; set one 'plane on fire and damaged at least four more. About twenty pom-poms all around the 'drome shot at us. There were four blue searchlights – damned accurate ones. They were mostly 88s on the deck – about eighteen, I should say; about a dozen 109s, probably more under camouflage netting, and about ten 215s, I think they were. Right, sir. We'll write the combat reports and get them 'phoned through to you. We'll be sleeping here. Thank you very much, sir. Good night."

"Ops are as pleased as Punch. You aren't to go tonight: the Met people say it's going to be foggy soon, Derek. We've got to write the reports, then we can push off to bed."

The intelligence officers turned up, and helped us write out our reports. Then, after a marvellous cup of tea, bed.

I lay in bed and thought. I wondered how many Huns we had killed that night: where on earth the Jerries had got all the guns from. Thank God for getting us home safely. We must win this war soon. Then . . .

Chapter 11

Buckingham Palace

I stayed up in the Cotswolds, flying to Exeter, every afternoon for the office work. The weather the night before had been bad, so we had got to bed early. As the sun was shining, I got up at ten. I thought a spot of riding would be good.

"Morning, 'Widge'. Seen the papers?" said Robbie as I walked into our breakfast-room.

"Morning, boys. What's in them? Has the war been won already, or is the invasion coming today, as usual?"

"Have a look, 'Widge'."

'Watty' chucked the *Daily Mail* at me. I glanced at the headlines. "Croydon Aerodrome Bombed. Dive-bombers Attacked Croydon. Little damage was done, and all enemy bombers destroyed before they left England."

"It's not on the front page, 'Widge'."

I turned the pages over. Hell's bells! List of R.A.F. awards: "The King has been graciously pleased to approve the following awards, which have been made in recognition of gallantry displayed in flying operations against the enemy." Distinguished Flying Cross. Third down of twelve names was mine.

"Suffering snakes! What will you drink, boys?"

"Damn good show, sir; you deserve it every time," Dickie said.

The boys showered me with congratulations. I was pleased – very pleased. I knew that my mother and Pamela would be very pleased.

"Well, boys, we'll have a bit of a party at lunch. Anybody got any money to lend me?"

The boys managed to produce a small sum which swelled my empty pockets. At lunch we had a spot of beer. The boys were very cheery. I could hardly realise that now I was entitled to wear the purple-and-white medal ribbon.

'I'll get one tomorrow at Exeter.'

I got grand telegrams from my family and Pamela. I was happy.

The Flights changed over, so I stayed at Exeter. "B" Flight boys had some good luck. They intercepted three Huns over Bristol about midnight and bashed them. They were all hit, but no confirmation was possible, as they must have crashed in the Bristol Channel. They were only counted as damaged. At Exeter everything remained very quiet. The Hun was still blitzing around London, but left our part of the world alone. We were very bored about it.

Then one afternoon we lost our Station Commander, Johnny. He had borrowed one of our machines to fly to Tangmere for a conference. He was in excellent spirits when he took off. Just after he had left, Ops told us that there was a blitz in that sector. They warned Johnny on the R.T. He gave the usual answer, "Message received and understood." Then nothing more. Johnny's body was washed up, riddled with bullets, five days later. We lost a grand Station Commander, and our friend.

Once more the Flights changed over. We were getting bored with no action. One afternoon I was sitting in the office with the Adjutant, having our usual three-o'clock cup of tea, when Ops 'phoned. "Huns coming across now." "O.K., Ops, I'll be out like a flash." "I'm off, Adj.; there's a blitz coming. See you anon." I bumped rapidly out to dispersal in the Ford.

Hell and damnation! Blue section of "B" Flight were up already. They had been sent off after a recco 'plane – presumably the Hun who had come across to look at the weather. He had presumably wirelessed back and said it was marvellous. It certainly was a fine, sunny afternoon – just right for a blitz.

"Well, John O'Toole, I haven't got the right frequency[41] in my wireless, so will you lead me?"

"O.K. sir. Hell! there's the 'phone."

"Hullo, Ops. Two 'planes only wanted? Plymouth. Hell! there's a raid going for Plymouth. Blast! Off you go, Mac and Connoly."

They hurtled off the deck.

"Well, John, old cock, that leaves us. I hope to hell the other Squadron know what they are up to."

We sit and wait, feeling the usual very empty feeling in the tummy. I 'phoned up Ops and asked them to send us off now. – "No; wait for orders." It was hell waiting, wondering whether we would be shot down. The sun somehow seemed to increase in heat just before a blitz. Anyway, there was some cloud about. A huge bank of cumulus towered over the eastern horizon. Yes, there was going to be plenty of cloud to hide in. That thought definitely cheered me. The 'phone rang.

"Start up. Patrol Portland."

I run like hell to my machine. Good boys! the engine is running. I jump in, straps on, then full throttle for a take-off, trailing a cloud of dust. As soon as I was air-borne I put my helmet on. My R.T. was useless, so I formated on John. We climbed flat out. Soon white clouds were flashing past our wing-tips; then we were above them, dodging down the large valleys between the towering white cloud-tops. The sun reflecting off the whiteness dazzled me.

'I sincerely hope that old John knows where he is. If his wireless packs, we'll get hopelessly lost.'

I slam the hood shut. It's not so hot now. I like the quietness when the hood is shut. I can always shoot better, and even though I sweat more, my mind is much cooler. I glanced at the altimeter – 12,000 feet.

---

[41] Each ground station operates on a different wireless wavelength.

Another 3,000 feet, then, suddenly John waggles his wings violently. What the hell does that mean? I weave hard and crane my neck, peering round the sky. 'Nothing. John is still waggling his wings. What on earth for? Why the hell haven't I got any R.T.? Blast it! Christ!' Over to my right, slightly above us, are two massive formations – bombers flying in perfect close formation.

I slammed the throttle wide open. Above the bombers, darting about like flies, are fighters. 'Damn them! why the hell haven't I got the Squadron with me? John has swung out to the left, climbing high. He seems to be making a bee-line for the fighters. Hell to that! the bombers will do me nicely. Hell! at this rate I'll never catch them. The swines have turned away. It's O.K., you'll make it yet.'

All the time I was weaving gently. High above the bombers I caught a glimpse now and then of the duck-egg blue of some friendly fighters; away to my right a 'plane goes vertically downwards, trailing a line of thick black smoke. Now I am about the right height. I swing out to the right flank. The Huns are most certainly putting up a pretty show. They are flying in neat vics, of three, sections of three, line abreast. Jerry aircraft always look beautifully new. These are no exception. The clean white paint round the black crosses shines in the sun. The right-hand last one will do me nicely. Now.

Brmmmmmmmm, brmmmmmmmmmmm.

Got him. Hell! The bomber falters, then banks over towards me. 'Christ! look out; you'll hit him. Oh God!' I catch a fleeting glimpse of the trailing edge. Stick forward. Blast! the engine's cut. Blast them! Every rear-gunner in the formation opened up. Bang, bang! bang, bang! Hell! they've hit me, the bastards. I'm going vertically downwards now. Above me the sky is criss-crossed by an absolute blanket of white tracer.

Over to my right the 88 that I attacked was spiralling downwards. Both hands on the stick, and I pull out of the dive. The bomber formation is about 8,000 feet above my head. The 88 disappeared in the cloud, still spiralling nearly vertically downwards. A glance at the compass shows that we are now heading south.

I start climbing again. There are packets to shoot at if only I can catch them. The controls feel O.K. Temperatures O.K. Two bullets have made neat holes in my right wing just outside the wing tank. Wonder where the hell John has got to? Blast these damned Jerries! they are going too damned fast. Speed, speed and more speed. Wonder where the hell I am? I sincerely hope I'm still over the land. I push against the throttle. It's no good pulling the tit, because I'm above 12,000.[42] 'I hope the hell that those swine up there don't see me.'

High above me the fighters are still circling. Slowly, very slowly, I'm gaining on them.

'Steady, 'Widge'; don't be a fool; turn back. No, go on. They're straggling a bit now. You can catch that straggler. 800 yards now. Be careful. Keep a damned good look-out behind. 600 yards. You won't hit me at that range.' About ten of the arse-end bombers are firing at me, missing me by miles: their tracer is disappearing beneath my nose. Hell! this is going to be damned unpleasant. The whole bomber formation appears to be going flat out; nearly everyone in the formation has black smoke coming from the engines.

My straggler was now about 300 yards behind the arse-end Charlie of the formation. Coming into range now. Steady sights on the rear-gunner, who is putting his tracer just by my hood. Brrrrrrmmmmmm. The return fire stopped. Brmmmmm, brmmmmmmmm. I slam the throttle shut. 'Christ! I'm over-shooting.'

The 88 falls away into a gentle dive; I give him another burst in the fuselage. The dive steepens – down, down.

'Is he hit or is he getting away? Christ!'

Suddenly, but rather slowly and gracefully, his wings come off, just where the engines are; simultaneously three black objects fly out from the top. Bodies. I was close enough to see them somersaulting.

---

[42] The extra boost does not increase speed above that height.

No parachutes open. The fuselage with the engines plunges vertically downwards, followed rather more slowly by the bodies, which recede into black dots. The wings flutter beneath me, falling like autumn leaves.

'Wake up, you fool! get out of this.'

Above me the fighters still dart across the sky. I aileron downwards, pulling out just on top of the clouds, and dive into the all-enveloping whiteness.

'Thank God! safe at last.'

I throttle back. All the instruments are haywire. I'm stone deaf; my ears hurt like hell as I squeeze and blow my nose. That's better – at least I can hear if the engine is going round. I steer due north, diving gently, 'Blast this cloud! it's damned thick.'

At last, I come out of it at 2,000 feet. Thank God for that! Over to my left is Portland Bill. Now I know where I am. Almost beneath me a large patch of fluorescence shows, where a pilot is in 'the drink'. I dive lower. There he is – theirs or ours Heaven knows. The motor-boats are speeding towards him.

I streak across the water, circle the leading boat and head back towards the pilot in the water. Then back again to the boat. The crew wave to me and give me the thumbs-up sign. They have seen the fluorescence. A final wave to them, and home. Once more I fly low over the cliffs, waving madly to anybody in the streets or fields. Hurrah! I'm still alive, and those bastard bombers have turned back. Thank God, there's the 'drome. A quick circuit and, for a change, a good landing.

Thank God there are a crowd of aircraft at "B" Flight – at least most of the boys are back.

"Hullo, sir! What did you get?" Ken asked as soon as I jumped from my cockpit.

"Two 88s – one confirmed and a probable. I ran into huge lots of 88s, flying in perfect formation. How many of the boys are back?"

"Everyone except Sergeant Connoly. He hasn't turned up yet. The boys have done well. Mac has got a 110 confirmed and an 88 damaged. John got an 88 confirmed and a 109 damaged. The other section hadn't caught their recco 'plane, and were very browned off, as they had had to refuel; eventually they had got off the deck again, but much too late."

"Wonder where the devil Connoly is? I hope he's O.K."

We sat around and chatted. The Jerries had evidently just crossed the coast, then turned round and headed straight back for France, without dropping many bombs – just a few in open country, presumably let go by Huns who had been attacked by our fighters.

After an hour Ops 'phoned up and said that Connoly was in Portland Hospital with shrapnel in his bottom, evidently not too badly hurt. He had been jumped on by two 109s just as he was about to shoot an 88. He hadn't even fired his guns when a cannon shell hit his cockpit, another one hit his glycol tank, so he baled out. He didn't realise that he was wounded until he landed and found that he couldn't walk. The Army shoved him in a car and took him to hospital.

"A" Flight were very annoyed that they had missed it. Mighty *Figaro* had got five bullet-holes in her: two through the wings and three up in the tail-plane. None of them had done any real damage; a dope-can and some small pieces of fabric was all that was needed to make her one hundred per cent serviceable.

"Here, 'Widge', your summons to Buckingham Palace has arrived," Dickie said.

He chucked me an official-looking letter. It contained a printed card, and an application form to return to the Lord Chamberlain requesting tickets for two relations or friends. "You are requested to attend a Levée to be held at 10.30 hours on the 19th of September 1940 at Buckingham Palace."

"What the hell is the date today – the 10th?"

"Steady on, 'Widge'; it's only the 8th," answered 'Watty'.

The days passed rapidly. The boys still roared up high after the elusive recco machines, and failed to get them. Generally, because the Hun saw them coming, he opened his throttles, shoved his nose down and fled.

The morning of the 18th dawned fine and sunny. I packed my suitcase and started the long drive to London. England was looking her best. The trees that lined the roads were heavy with leaves. Except for army huts and camouflaged lorries parked in fields, it might have been any peaceful autumn. I was happy driving up. The car was going well; the sun shining on the countryside cheered and warmed my heart. England, with all her faults, was definitely worth fighting for.

The miles sped by. Soon I was racing up the Great West Road. I had expected to see many bombed factories; there wasn't one: the first bomb-damage that I saw was at the first roundabout, where the smallest shops had received a direct hit. The sight of the rubble reminded me of France. How different the English were from the French! Why? Heaven only knows.

My family were having tea in the garden when I arrived at our house. Pamela was there, looking divine. My Pam, you are a wonderful inspiration to me. It was grand being home again. Sitting in deck chairs in the garden reminded me of my holidays from school. In this hell and filth of war it was wonderful being really happy.

My mother and father were coming to watch the investiture, while Daphne, my sister, and Pam stayed outside. Then we were having a party at the Savoy with some friends of the family. Another fine day, was my first thought as I woke to see my room bathed in streaming sunlight. Then I realised where I was. Hell! today I was collecting my gong.[43] I hadn't realised it before, but now I felt nervous about the whole proceeding. Breakfast flashed by, and there we were clambering into the big hired Daimler. "Have you got the tickets?" my mother asked just as we started. I felt in my pockets. "Yes, darling – yours and my own."

---

[43] R.A.F. slang for D.F.C. or any other medal.

Of course, we arrived about half an hour early, so we stopped in the Park and waited. I paced up and down, feeling in an awful sweat.

Should I leave my top button undone? Having the top button undone is one of those unwritten traditions that my Squadron had always kept up. I will leave my button undone. The minutes ticked slowly by. Quite a few Service men were walking towards the Palace. "Come on, Ian; it's time we started moving," my father said.

We drove slowly towards the Palace. There was quite a traffic jam – taxis and private cars bunched round the gates. The sentries, in ordinary battle-dress, were standing stiffly at attention. At the gates two extra sentries were inspecting the tickets. I showed them ours, and we drove into the huge courtyard. The car was allowed to park there. Out we got and joined quite a long queue of Naval, Army and Air Force officers of all ranks, and crowds of elderly men and women – the parents.

As soon as we entered the wide doors a footman motioned the crowd of parents to the seats in the adjoining room. We, the service blokes, queued up at a counter, where we left our hats, gas-masks and coats. We were told to keep our gloves with us, and were escorted to another room by an usher, who took our names, carefully noting them down. This was the waiting-room.

It was large and square, hung with oil paintings of past monarchs. There were about fifty people in the room; all the services were represented, including some very tough-looking Merchant Navy skippers. We stood around talking. I found several old acquaintances. I thought, as I chatted to them, of all my friends who had died. Many had deserved medals, but had not lived long enough to have them awarded. We stood around for what seemed hours – actually about half an hour. We were mostly cracking jokes. The room had filled up since I had come in. There were quite a sprinkling of civilians dressed in morning coats. Many of them were knighted by the King.

At last, the chief usher reappeared and called for silence. "Please answer your names and line up here." The roll call started. We lined up – D.S.Os. first, then the oddments, the civilians, then D.F.Cs., D.F.Ms. There were a few absentees. I wondered if they were dead.

At last, we lined up in three lines and the show started. After we were in line, we were told what we had to do. "Step up on to the dais, halt, turn left, and bow. Not from the waist, but just nod your heads. The King will then place the medal on these clips." The clips were handed out to us and we pinned them on to our tunics, just beneath our wings in the case of the R.A.F. These clips enabled the King to place the medal on without the difficult job of pinning it. "After the medal is on, turn right and march down to the vestibule, where a footman at a counter will give you boxes to put your medals in and hand in the clips."

The doors were opened, and we started a slow shuffle along the passage. An orchestra was now playing at the back of the audience. After about five minutes my part of the queue moved round the corner, and we could see what was happening. The King was standing on the raised dais. An Army officer and several Naval officers were standing just behind him. A very senior Naval officer had the list of names and was calling them out.

Hollywood, in one of its most magnificent films, could not have got a better lighting effect. His Majesty looked very well and sunburnt – very much like his pictures, but more handsome than the average photo. He was in naval uniform. The gold braid on his arm reached nearly to his elbow. A civilian mounted the dais. He knelt, and the King touched each shoulder with a sword. So that is how one is knighted. It came as a decided shock when I found that there were only three more people to go in front of me. My parents were sitting well in the front of the audience. I gave them a swift wink. The orchestra started another tune. They looked rather out of place in their army battle-dress. They were all members of the Palace Home Guard.

My name was called out. I stepped on to the dais, turned left and made a gentle bow. "Congratulations. I hope that we shall see you here again soon." The King neatly placed the glittering silver cross on my breast. I stepped back, turned right and marched briskly down to the foyer.

The footman handed me a small jeweller's box, and placed my medal in it. We now stood and looked through the doors and watched the others being decorated. At last, the last one was done. The orchestra gave a roll of drums. The audience rose and "God Save the King" was sung, His Majesty standing at attention. Then the King said "Good morning", and turned and walked through the doors at the back of the dais. The investiture was over.

We queued up again for our hats and gas-masks. I found my parents, and we walked into the spacious courtyard. Footmen were dashing about trying to find cars. "Sir Thomas Brown's car," one called. "I dunno about any Sir Thomas Brown – I'm Mr. Brown's shuvver," said the driver of a big Rolls.

We found our car O.K. and drove out. There was a crowd at the gates, including press photographers. On the whole it was one of the most impressive ceremonies that I have ever attended. It gave me courage and increased my morale. Nazis, you may blow London and every town in our country to smithereens – if you can. You shall never rule the British Isle.

Chapter 12

The Work Goes On

Back to work, after an excellent lunch at the Savoy. Dinner at Grosvenor House, and several happy hours at the grand play *Cottage to Let*. The next morning, after swift farewells, I tore down the Great West Road, across Salisbury Plain, back to work at Exeter.

The daylight attacks on England ceased. The Huns had had enough. The R.A.F. definitely ruled the skies of England in the day-time, but not at night. The Squadron was ordered to have one flight always night-flying. Robbie, Derek and I agreed that the best way of doing that was for the flights to do week and week about. The boys liked that combination, one week night-flying and the next week at Exeter day-flying. We didn't realise at the time that we should see the Luftwaffe over this country again.

The moon rose again – the moon that the night-flier almost worships. Our offensive spirit rose. I arranged more ground-straffs with Group. On one of these Derek and 'Bea' were first, 'Rubber' and I were doing the second straff. The night was fine with a good weather forecast. This time we were going for another 'drome, on the Cherbourg peninsula. Not so bad. It was strangely warm for an autumn evening. We were all in high spirits. The dinner was good. We lay around in the mess and read books, wrote letters, even played quite good games of ping-pong, but we did not attempt anything on the billiard-tables. I think we were all rather frightened that we would tear the cloth.

As usual, the minutes seemed like hours. At last, the time came for us to go out and warm the machines up. It was nearly as bright as day.

Everything was set. Permission to go off granted, 'Bea' and Derek clambered into their machines. I strapped Derek in.

"Good luck, Derek; don't be too reckless. We'll let the Verey lights off for you this time."

I pressed the starter battery button, the engines roared into life; they taxied out to the flare-path and were off. Their silhouette against the moon gave me an odd thrill. 'Rubber' and I walked back to the hut. It would be about an hour and a half's wait. 'God! I hope that everything will be O.K.'

We kicked our heels and read our books. There seemed nothing much to talk about. Every ten minutes or so I walked outside to look at the weather. The moon shone down from the clear sky like some sphinx; the stars were very bright. 'What an incredible world it is! As I stand here people all over Europe are dying. Some Jerries, who really most likely are quite decent chaps, will be dead soon. Killed by a fighter flown by a young New Zealander who has gone half-way round the world to fly against the Nazi swine. You fools! do you really think you have got a hope, with all your Aryan blood and master race? Somehow England is a symbol that you will never crush.'

'Rubber' was nervous: I could tell it by the way he cracked his bad jokes. I felt heavy with responsibility. 'Bea' and Derek should be O.K., but 'Rubber' had only joined us just after France, and hadn't done nearly as many hours' flying. Don't worry, he is keen and well trained. An hour passed; the weather still very fine. All would be well.

"Come on, 'Rubber'; we'll warm our machines up; then we'll be all set as soon as we've got the dope from Ops."

We warmed the machines up. Everything was O.K. in my machine, but 'Rubber's' generator was U.S., so he changed his helmet over to Peter's machine. Now, if only they will come back, we'll be all set. Another ten minutes and they should be here. Thank God for this weather! It's perfect for the job. We stood outside the hut, Verey pistol in hand, staring at the southern sky, listening. Silence except for the gentle breeze singing through the trees. "Shhhhh! do you hear what I hear?"

Very faintly I heard the throb of an engine. Quickly it became louder. "That's a 'Hurry' all right; what about giving him a green?" 'Rubber' said. – "No, let's wait a bit: he should be able to find the 'drome without it." The hum of the engine grew louder. "There he is." The navigation lights of a 'plane suddenly appear in the sky nearly overhead. "He's found us O.K. He's signalling for permission to land. Wonder who it is?" The aldis lamp at the end of the flare-path flashes green. The 'plane does a tight circuit, then comes into land.

As soon as it has turned off from the flare-path we flash our torches at it to show the pilot where to taxi. "It's 'Bea'." We crowd round the 'plane.

"How did you get on?" I asked.

"O.K., sir. There are about thirty 109s in the 'drome, some of them parked very close together. I'm certain I bashed two of them. The blasted searchlights were damned unpleasant. There were six of them. Only three were shining when I left. Derek's O.K.: he called me up on the way home. The pom-poms were bloody. I've never been so frightened in my life. Honestly, they came so close they dazzled me. I beat up several of the gun-posts and stopped them firing. It was O.K. We left plenty of aircraft for you to crack at, sir."

"Damned good show, 'Bea'. There's Derek." The noise of another engine broke the silence. "Thank God for that! I don't pick this sitting on the ground waiting."

Derek landed quickly. I jumped up on to his wing as soon as he taxied in.

"Good show, Derek! How did you get on?"

"It was wizard, old boy – showers of 109s parked in neat lines; but the flak was hellish hot. I managed to get a good burst in at a line of 109s before anybody fired a shot at us. After that it was like a colossal firework display. The bloody searchlights fixed me good and proper. After that I tore around shooting up the gun-posts. Unless they have got showers of spare crews, I don't think many of the guns will fire at you. I managed to ding them as they were firing at you, 'Bea'. Good show smacking those searchlights. They certainly had me foxed."

"Derek, old boy, draw us a diagram of the 'drome, showing where the aircraft are, and we'll push off. What's the weather like over there?"

"It's absolutely grand. You can't miss the 'drome. It shows up as a huge square light patch."

We went into the Watch-hut, and Derek showed us carefully where the 'planes were, and rough positions of gun-posts and searchlights.

"What's happening over here? Something burning up north?" – "I don't know; Ops say there are quite a lot of Huns about. Well, Derek, we'll push off."

'Rubber' and I walked out to our 'planes.

"Good luck, 'Rubber'. Don't forget what I've told you: don't go too low; and keep turning after you've attacked."

"O.K., sir; good luck. I'll give you a call on the R.T. on the way home."

We clambered into the cockpits; Derek strapped me in this time.

"Smash them, 'Widge'. See you in an hour and a half." The engine started O.K. I taxied out, followed closely by 'Rubber'. 'Please God let everything be O.K.' As soon as I left the ground, I throttled back to economical cruising speed. 'Rubber' appeared on my left in close formation. As we crossed the coast, I switched the navigation lights off.

We climbed gently. I concentrated hard on the compass, then looked up and found a convenient star that was slap in the middle of the windscreen. That would do to steer by. England faded behind us. Below, the sea shone silver in the moon. It looked very beautiful. 'God, I hope I don't drop in it. Oh, Christ, I've forgotten my torch! Still, I hope to hell I don't need it.' I turned on the reflector sight, dimmed it with the rheostat and switched it off. Everything seemed O.K. I flashed O.K. on my recognition light to 'Rubber'. Back came his answer – O.K. I closed the lid. It was a bit chilly flying.

We levelled out at 10,000. I stared at the star, glancing down at the compass now and then to check. I glanced often at the cockpit clock. We had left the ground at one fifty. It was now exactly two. Another ten minutes and we should be there. 'Everything will be all right. I'm sure everything will be all right.

Christ! a 'plane. It was lightly above me, coming straight towards me. I shoved the stick hard over and swung into a steep right-hand turn. Full throttle. Steady! There it is – doing a left-hand turn. I throttle back and follow it round. It straightened up and flew straight again. I glanced at the compass. Due north. 'Now steady; get a bit closer and have a look at what it is. Twin rudders, straight wings, radial engines. Dornier 17z.'

'Steady now; you're over half-way across the Channel. No place to have a fight. Just stay where you are until the shores of dear old England loom up, then give him the works. Christ! wonder where 'Rubber' has got to? Hope he hasn't spun in. He'll be all right. Throttle open a bit – you're getting too far behind. That's better. Steady; you're getting too close. Blast this long-range formation! I don't pick it at all. This is a piece of cake. I'll wait until we are crossing the coast, then open fire.'

I turned the reflector sight on. 'Now what the hell is the span of a 17? God knows, I don't.' 70 feet will do. I twisted the range-finder round, set the range to 250 yards, and I was all set.

'Damn! you're over-shooting again.'

I strained my eyes, trying to keep not too close, yet not to lose sight of it.

'Close up, you fool! you're getting miles too far behind.' I slammed the throttle open. The black blur that was the Hun 'plane suddenly loomed up, black and clear. 'Hell! you've overshot.' I was practically underneath him now. I slammed the throttle shut. Too much so. Streaks of flame spurted from my exhausts. 'Blast!' Twin streaks of tracer whipped over my head.

'He's seen me. Right! Give him the works.'

I opened the throttle, sights on, and gave him a short burst. Nothing happened. 'Blast!'

Brrmmmmm. 'Got him.'

I saw flashes all along his fuselage. He was turning and started diving.

'Sights on again. This time a half-deflection shot.'

Brrrrrrmmmmmm.

A burst of flame jumped from the starboard engine.

Brmmmmmm. It flickered and spread along the wing. A shower of sparks flew back. The top rear-gunner was still firing, but missing badly.

I gave him another burst, and the return fire stopped. I ceased fire and watched. The 'plane was doing a gentle diving turn, round, round and round. The fire in the right wing grew bigger; burning pieces started falling from it. It was a fascinating sight, silhouetted against the sea; the fire flared up and lit up the fuselage. Round and round. I glanced at the altimeter. Two thousand feet; and, going down, I could see the waves now. No one had baled out. Now he's going in. For a second, he looked as if he had pulled up, then he touched, bounced, touched again, showers of sparks flying off the engine, then hit with a shower of spray. I steep-turned, and caught sight of the tail standing boldly up.

'Whew, that's that! Now for home.'

I climbed up and turned north.

'Good show! there's the coast.'

I switched the R.T. on to transmit. "Hullo, Pierot! Foible leader calling. One bandit shot down in sea about ten miles out. Over."

Rather faintly came their reply, "Pierot calling. Good show Foible leader. Message received. Over."

I crossed the coast. It was high cliffs. 'Where the hell am I?'

After five minutes of studying the map, I found that I was only about fifteen miles from the 'drome. I turned west and soon picked it up. Well, that was short and sweet and damned easy.

I switched the nav.[44] lights on and swung in to land. That really was easy. I taxied rapidly to the dispersal point and switched off.

"What's wrong, 'Widge'?" was Derek's anxious enquiry.

"Nothing, old boy. I've just knocked a Dornier 17 into 'the drink', only about ten miles out. I met it half-way across, did a swift turn, and got on to its tail. Is there any sign of 'Rubber'? He must have had a hell of a shock."

"There he is now." A 'plane roared low across the 'drome.

"Good show, 'Widge'! You are a lucky devil."

'Rubber' taxied in and jumped out of his cockpit.

"What on earth went into 'the drink'? God, sir! it gave me a shock. I thought it was you. One moment you were there, sir, and the next you had disappeared."

"I'm sorry, 'Rubber'. I suddenly saw a hulking great Hun, so turned and chased him. It was he who dropped in 'the drink': he bounced exactly like a flat, skimming stone."

"Congrats, sir; that's just grand!"

"Ops want you on the 'phone."

"Hullo, Ops. Yes, thanks a lot; I'm pleased about that. I didn't see anyone get out; they might have done. The rescue-boats are going out. No more tonight. Mist forming. O.K., sir. Good night. – That was the Group Controller."

"The coastguards have confirmed my Jerry – they saw it go in. They've got a good fix on it, and are sending out a boat, just in case there are some survivors. We aren't to go across again, as it's going to be misty here soon. So, we can all push off to bed."

No survivors were picked up.

The Squadron is on full-time night-flying now, and looks forward to giving a very hot reception to any Hun that comes over this country

---

[44] Navigation lights.

of ours. So far in this war we have knocked down 135 Huns confirmed, probably destroyed 47 more, and damaged 42.

Sixteen of my comrades have died to achieve this, some through enemy action and some through flying accidents. They have left behind them very happy memories.

Postscript

'Widge' had been promoted to acting flight lieutenant on 7 November 1939, being posted to the newly formed 266 Squadron at Sutton Bridge as a flight commander, flying Spitfires. Four days after Hitler invaded the West, Flight Lieutenant Gleed was sent across the Channel to join 87 Squadron in France. Over the next week, in a battle already lost, he destroyed seven enemy aircraft – becoming an ace – and probably destroyed another. It was an impressive start to his personal war.

After the Fall of France, 87 Squadron rested at Debden and Church Fenton before settling at Exeter in 10 Group. It was from there, and Bibury in Gloucestershire, under the leadership of firstly Wing Commander Johnny Dewar DSO, DFC, and then Squadron Leader 'Widge' Gleed, that the unit would fight during the Battle of Britain. During that epic aerial conflict of summer 1940, 'Widge' added to his score four more enemy aircraft destroyed, two probables and another damaged. Indeed, his DFC, awarded for his efforts in France, was gazetted on 13 September 1940. The citation reads:

> Flight Lieutenant Gleed took over a flight in 87 Squadron on arriving from England after intensive hostilities had begun. The Squadron was moved several times, and he knew neither the officers or the airmen. He took on his task with energy and discretion, won the confidence of his flight and led them with skill and success. In his very first patrol his flight was engaged by greatly superior numbers of enemy fighters and he accounted for two

Me 110s. Throughout he showed great courage in the air
and was on duty almost continuously.

It was a well-deserved award. What is perhaps surprising, however, is
that a Bar was not awarded for his Battle of Britain efforts. Clearly,
though, 'Widge' Gleed was not only an exceptional fighter pilot – he
was a natural leader of equal merit.

By the end of September 1940, the *Luftwaffe*, unable to continue
sustaining such heavy losses to its bomber force, switched its
bombers, and in particular the Heinkel He 111, completely to
night-bombing. At that time, Britain's nocturnal defences remained
primitive; dedicated night-fighting aircraft were only just starting to
arrive and airborne interception radar was still being developed. This
made nocturnal operations safer for the Germans, the trade-off being
less accurate bombing.

Although both the Spitfire and Hurricane were designed and
intended as day fighters, such was the urgency of the hour that both
types were pressed into a stop-gap night-fighting role, for which,
with a wider track undercarriage, the latter proved more suited. These
'Fighter Nights', however, achieved comparatively little success, and
this was certainly 87 Squadron's experience operating from both
Colerne and Charmy Down during the winter of 1940/41, when the
night Blitz was at its terrible height.

Significantly, though, by March 1941, the Spitfire Mk.II was
replacing the Hurricane as the RAF's frontline day-fighter, and Fighter
Command had been re-organised into three-squadron-strong wings,
based at sector stations. All of this was geared up to the so-called
'Non-Stop Offensive' of 1941, during which Fighter Command
adopted an aggressive posture, reaching out and taking the war across
the Channel to the Germans in northern France.

No.87 Squadron retained its Hurricanes, however, as a specialist
night-flying unit, called upon to undertake intruder operations after
dark against enemy airfields across the sea. Flying at night in those

days was far from easy, the blackout denying pilots a ground reference, and these were highly dangerous, low-level affairs.

During this period of operations, 'Widge' destroyed two more enemy aircraft, and probably destroyed another, in addition to destroying a Do 17 (shared with Flight Lieutenant Rayner) and damaging four other German machines on the ground during strafing attacks on *Luftwaffe* airfields. This was, without a doubt, highly skilful flying. Given 'Widge's experience, however, it is no surprise that, on 18 November 1941, he was promoted to acting wing commander and posted to lead the Spitfire wing based at 10 Group's Middle Wallop Sector Station. This was, of course, every fighter pilot's dream job: the Wing Commander (Flying) was unfettered by administration and solely responsible for the operational and fighting efficiency of his three squadron-strong wing.

All through the air-fighting 'season' of 1941, which had concluded on 8 November 1941, Fighter Command had flown a relentless round of offensive operations, including bomber escort missions, codenamed 'Circus', and 'Rhubarbs', in which pairs of fighters flew very low, so as to avoid detection by German radar, shooting-up targets of opportunity, attacks on enemy shipping, and fighter sweeps.

Following Hitler's invasion of Russia on 22 June 1941, these operations, which actually achieved little or nothing from a strategic perspective, became highly political as the western Allies strove to prove to the Soviets that everything was being done to support them by tying down German units on the Channel coast. In truth, north-west France remained defended by two German fighter groups throughout the war, which were not reinforced by units from the east, while Fighter Command lost many highly experienced fighter leaders and pilots during these intensive operations. Moreover, there was a new threat in the Focke-Wulf Fw 190, which was faster than the Spitfire Mk.VB then in service, although the Spitfire could out-turn the new German fighter. Clearly, there were interesting times ahead for Wing Commander Gleed and his Middle Wallop Wing.

'Widge's next kill, however, was not until 13 March 1942, when he shared a Ju 88 'probable' off Portland; a Ju 88 plunged into the sea off the same landmark six days later. On 17 April 1942, Wing Commander Gleed and Squadron Leader 'Bunny' Currant shared an Me 109F 'probable' over France, and after further victories 'Widge' scored his sole success against the Fw 190 in the form of a 'probable' over Hardelot on 5 May 1942.

Gleed's award of the DSO was gazetted on 22 May 1942. The citation states:

> This officer has led his Wing on twenty-six sorties over enemy territory. He has always displayed a fine fighting spirit which combined with his masterly leadership and keenness has set an inspiring example. Wing Commander Gleed has destroyed at least twelve enemy aircraft, two of which he shot down at night.

'Widge' was now the proud recipient of the 'double': the DSO and DFC.

Wing Commander Gleed, who had flown operationally without rest since 3 September 1939, would not, however, see out the 'season' that year. He was posted as a staff officer to HQ Fighter Command (Tactics) on 16 July 1942, then moved over to Operations, also at Bentley Priory, that December.

On New Year's Day 1943, 'Widge' was posted to the Western Desert, and initially attached to 145 Squadron, to assimilate to Desert Air Force (DAF) operating conditions. He was appointed to command 244 Wing on 31 January 1943.

By this time, the Allies had landed in Algiers and victory in North Africa now appeared on the cards. Early in 1943, Field Marshal Montgomery reached Tripoli, his ground forces closely supported by Air Vice-Marshal 'Mary' Coningham's DAF, which had achieved great results in tactical air cooperation. The fighter-bombers importance in this theatre is confirmed by the DAF's order of battle, comprising two such wings, with another in reserve, and only one of fighters: 244.

Gleed's new, mainly Spitfire-equipped, command was responsible for maintaining aerial supremacy over the battlefield, enabling the fighter-bombers to do their work, and consisted of 92, 145 and 601 RAF squadrons, 1 South African Air Force Squadron, and the night-fighting Hurricanes of 73 Squadron. In the DAF, though, the wing leader's role was different to back in 'Blighty'. In the Western Desert, the wing commander had full responsibility for his formation, including administration; operational flying was the senior squadron commander's domain. Nonetheless, typically, Wing Commander Gleed would lead from the cockpit, not the desk.

The award of a Belgian *Croix de Guerre* was gazetted on 15 February 1943:

> A senior officer of great bravery and outstanding competence. The Leader of a unit of several Belgian pilots, he led them to battle through several offensives over enemy occupied territory, inspiring them with the example of his drive and devotion to duty.

With the Allied armies on the offensive, 'Widge' damaged a Me 109F near Medinine on 7 March 1943, destroyed a 109G over the German frontline ten days later, and, on 6 April, damaged another 109F. It would be his last combat success.

With the end in Tunisia well in sight, Wing Commander Gleed briefed pilots at the Goubrine South Landing Ground on 16 April 1943. Axis forces grimly hung on, however, reliant upon transport aircraft ferrying in supplies, especially fuel. Standing patrols off Cap Bon were therefore arranged in the hope of Allied fighters intercepting these transports, and the German fighters were equally determined to ensure the safe arrival of these essential supplies. The area off Cap Bon, therefore, became a veritable hornets' nest.

That afternoon, Wing Commander Gleed led a patrol, at the head of 145 Squadron, in the hope of intercepting these precious enemy cargoes, whilst a section of 92 Squadron, led by the ace Flight Lieutenant Neville Duke DSO, DFC, provided high cover. Over the Mediterranean, it was Duke who spotted the enemy transports first, which 'Widge' was unable to see from his lower vantage point.

Wisely, the Wing Leader ordered 92 Squadron to lead the attack, whilst he and 145 followed. Duke's Spitfires were soon in action against a formation of eighteen German Ju 52s and Italian SM82s – whilst the Me 109s of JG77, and several Fw 190s, rained down upon 145 Squadron. Rapidly, Flight Sergeant Rostant's Spitfire was in flames, the pilot baling out, and Duke was calling for assistance. The sky was full of twisting and turning fighters, and a confused combat developed.

Back at Goubrine, there was one other Spitfire missing: Wing Commander Gleed's clipped wing Mk.V, AB502. Exactly what happened to 'Widge' will never be known, but Leutnant Reinert and Leutnant Berres both claimed Spitfires in the engagement, although it impossible to say from the information available which one was Wing Commander Gleed's.

Although a patrol was quickly flown off the Tunisian coast in the hope of finding Wing Commander Gleed alive and bobbing around in his dinghy, the sad fact was that the twenty-six-year-old 'Wizard Midget' had crashed on land and was dead.

Today, the grave of Wing Commander Ian Richard Gleed DSO, DFC can be found at Enfidaville Military Cemetery in Tunisia. Posthumously, in 1946, a French *Croix de Guerre* was added to his decorations.

His friend, Squadron Leader Laurence 'Rubber' Thorogood DFC once told me that '"Widge" was an amazing little chap, so energetic and enthusiastic, and such a great pilot; a natural leader, I never knew one better. It was a sad loss when he was killed.'

Further words would be superfluous.

The Thorogood Photograph Album

According to 'Widge' Gleed, when 87 Squadron re-formed at Church Fenton in June 1940, after the Fall of France, receiving replacement pilots and aircraft, 'We ... nicknamed one of our new pilots "Rubber", because he bounced.' The name stuck.

Squadron Leader Laurence Arthur 'Rubber' Thorogood DFC certainly survived some scrapes, including an incident during training at Brize Norton earlier that month: 'My engine cut and by some lucky chance I made a successful wheels-down landing in a small field in the Cotswolds – result: "Above average" rating as a pilot – what jam!!'

'Rubber' actually epitomised a generation of young men provided an opportunity to fly owing to the Second World War, one that may not have otherwise presented itself. Unlike so many of his contemporaries, 'Rubber' fortunately survived.

In 1996 'Rubber' gave me access to his album of unique snapshots. Taken mostly by himself, others by Flying Officer Rafael 'Watty' Watson, these revealed his time with 87 Squadron between June 1940 and April 1942. During wartime, personal photography, especially on service installations, was prohibited – which makes all of these rare windows on the past all the more valuable to the historic record.

Not, of course, that 'Rubber' and friends had this in mind at the time; as Supermarine test pilot Jeffrey Quill once said to me: 'Dear boy, our minds were not focussed on posterity in 1940.' As 'Rubber' himself said, 'We were having a hoot!' Be that as it may, this collection of photographs really is remarkable.

'Rubber' was born in Letchworth, Hertfordshire, on 13 May 1919, and was inspired by his father – 'who built an aircraft in 1910 but ran out of cash and couldn't afford to buy the engine' – to become an aviation enthusiast. An apprentice engineer at Luton, in 1938, 'Rubber' joined the RAF Volunteer Reserve. This was a far-sighted initiative and component of the 1936 Expansion Plan, one that was based upon local centres and the 'citizen volunteer' principle. Volunteers remained in their civilian occupations, studying ground subjects during certain weekday evenings, and learned to fly at weekends. The idea was that in the event of a crisis these men, all having completed elementary flying training, could be mobilised to increase the RAF's establishment and provided further, advanced, service flying training before posting to operational squadrons.

At the time, RAF Cranwell trained the service's professional officers, whose numbers were increased through the SSC scheme, the Auxiliary Air Force (AAF) and University Air Squadrons providing a further trained reserve. When the Second World War broke out, the RAFVR was mobilised, that is to say called to full-time service, at which point the reservist aircrew all automatically became sergeants – causing some resentment amongst pre-war professional airmen, given how long, under normal circumstances, it took to achieve this exulted non-commissioned rank.

After service flying training, some reservists were commissioned immediately, for others it took longer. As Air Vice-Marshal Johnnie Johnson said, 'The VR was a great thing, enabling grammar school boys to fly, whereas the Auxiliary Air Force was entirely focussed upon public schoolboys, as were Permanent, and to a large degree Short Service, Commissions before the war. And in those days, although as part of the Expansion Plan some NCOs were able to fly, the numbers of non-commissioned pilots were small. It was the VR, really, that made the whole thing more accessible, and accelerated the junior service becoming more of a meritocracy.'

Johnnie, of course, was himself an RAFVR pilot, rejected by the AAF on account of his comparatively humble social background, who became the RAF's official top-scoring fighter pilot of the war. So, for the aviation-minded likes of Johnnie and 'Rubber', the RAFVR offered a unique opportunity to fly – which was eagerly seized.

Having successfully completed ab initio flying training at Ansty, 'Rubber' was flying Hawker Hart biplane fighters at Luton when war broke out. Mobilised, Sergeant Thorogood reported to 1 Initial Training Wing at Cambridge University's Pembroke College, for an induction to service life. He reported to 2 Flying Training School at Brize Norton in March 1940, receiving the coveted RAF pilot's brevet there on 25 April. Having converted to Hurricanes, 'Rubber' reported to 87 Squadron, then commanded by Squadron Leader Johnny Dewar DSO, DFC, at Church Fenton on 18 June 1940. A replacement pilot, he joined Flight Lieutenant 'Widge' Gleed's 'A' Flight.

After the unit moved south to Exeter, 'Rubber' damaged a Ju 87 on 19 July, and destroyed a Ju 88 on 25 August 1940. On 24 May 1941, together with 'Widge', now commanding 87 Squadron, he shared a Do 18 flying boat, and participated in night intruder operations over northern France.

Commissioned on 14 August 1941, 'Rubber' was eventually posted away on rest in April 1942, following which he served in the Far East. Remaining in the post-war RAF, he eventually retired in 1964, and left us for blue skies in 2005.

Fortunately, his collection of photographs serves to remind us of those heady days when, as a young man, 'Rubber' flew Hurricanes in anger alongside the 'Wizard Midget'.

Sergeant Laurence Arthur 'Rubber' Thorogood whilst serving at Bibury, Gloucestershire, with 87 Squadron during the Battle of Britain.

Above: Practising blind-flying at Brize Norton on the Link Trainer.

Right: Resting at Brize Norton during training.

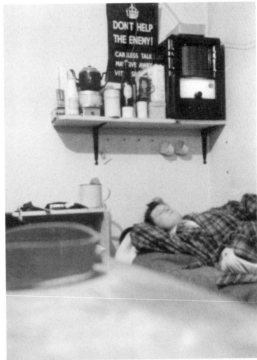

Flight Lieutenant 'Widge' Gleed at Exeter, August 1940.

'Widge' in his famous, red-nosed Hurricane, LK-A, P2978. No.87 Squadron's aircraft were all adorned by Disney characters, in this case 'Figaro' the cat.

'Rubber' in P2978.

Above: 'Rubber' at Bibury in his own Hurricane, sporting 'Pluto' the Disney dog.

Left: Squadron Leader Johnny Dewar DSO, DFC snapped at Exeter in July 1940. Dewar would soon be promoted to wing commander and become Exeter's Station Commander. He was reported missing in transit to Tangmere on 11 September 1940, having run into an incoming German raid over Southampton. An exceptional airman and leader, Wing Commander Dewar's body was washed ashore a few days later. The highest-ranking officer to die in the Battle of Britain, his grave can be found at St John the Baptist, North Baddesley, near Southampton.

The popular Johnny Dewar was succeeded in command of 87 Squadron by a New Zealander, Squadron Leader Terence Gunion Lovell-Gregg – universally known as 'Shuvvel'. Sadly, Lovel-Gregg was killed in action during his first engagement on 15 August 1940, and lies at rest, a long way from home, in Warmwell Churchyard, Dorset. Coincidentally, the pilot behind his CO is Flying Officer Ken Tait, also a New Zealander. Reported missing on 4 August 1941, Tait has no known grave.

Above: 'Rubber's' fellow photography enthusiast on 87 Squadron was Flying Officer 'Watty' Watson, pictured here, on the extreme right, at Exeter with pilot friends and his collection of scale flying models. From the left are: 'Rubber'; two Belgians, Pilot Officers Francois de Spirlet and Roger Malengrau; and New Zealander Pilot Officer Ken Tait. Neither de Spirlet nor Tait survived the war.

Left: Flying Officer Watson, with ever-present camera, enjoys some off-duty time afloat off the Isles of Scilly in 1941.

Sergeant Francis Vincent 'Dinkie' Howell at Bibury. A veteran of the Battle of France, Howell survived being shot down and recorded several victories over France and during the Battle of Britain. He passed away in 1984.

Some of 87 Squadron's Hurricanes at Exeter.

'Widge' and 'A' Flight pilots at the famous Swan Hotel in Bibury, Gloucestershire, in August 1940. Snapped by 'Rubber' on Watson's camera, they are, from the left, Flying Officer Watson, Pilot Officer Tait, 'Widge', Flying Officer Roddy Rayner (referred to as 'Robbie' in Gleed's book), and Pilot Officer Peter Comely. The latter was reported missing off Portland on 15 August 1940. He has no known grave.

Sergeant 'Rubber' Thorogood and his Hurricane, accumulator trolly plugged in, ready to go at Bibury during August 1940.

'Rubber' at immediate readiness at Bibury in a very weathered Hurricane.

'Rubber' in the cockpit at Bibury. He was pictured with his (unfortunately anonymous) engine fitter and rigger/radio mechanic.

'Rubber' with a 'bent' Hurricane at Bibury. 'These are of no interest', he wrote, 'because I crashed it!'.

Another view of the 'bent' Hurricane at Bibury.

A close-up of the 'prang' at Bibury.

Flying Officer Watson and Corporal McNaulty at Bibury.

Above: Flying Officer Roddy Rayner relaxing at Bibury.

Left: 'Rubber' outside a bell tent at Bibury.

A view of 87 Squadron's dispersal at Bibury.

Flying Officer Derek Ward, another New Zealander serving with 87 Squadron, pictured at Bibury with his Hurricane, LK-P, named *Kia Ora*. Ward survived the Battle of Britain, becoming a successful fighter pilot and leader who was decorated with a double DFC. Sadly, he was killed in action over the western desert on 17 June 1942 – a victim of Oberleutnant Hans-Joachim Marseille of JG27 – '*Der Stern von Afrika*' (Star of Africa).

One of a series of images showing 'Rubber' demonstrating the process of baling out. In reality, the procedure was to open the canopy, invert the aircraft, remove the safety harness locking pin – and simply drop out. As 'Rubber' said, 'How to bale out: if you have time!'

A second image taken during 'Rubber's' demonstration. As he himself one said, 'How to bale out: if you have time!'

Above: The last of our series of photographs taken during 'Rubber's' display revealing how to bale out.

Right: Flying Officer Ken Tait pictured at Exeter.

Above: An unknown 87 Squadron pilot prepares for flight at Exeter.

Left: Sergeant Cowley, 'Rubber' and Flying Officer Rody Rayner at Exeter, with a Triumph Dolomite 'personal transport'.

Sergeant James Cowley, who had re-mustered from rigger to pilot. Shot down and wounded on 15 August 1940, Cowley survived the war.

'Widge' (right) with Pilot Officer Peter Comely at Exeter dispersal, July 1940.

The 'office' in one of 87 Squadron's Hurricanes.

Flying Officer Watson overseeing the harmonisation of the guns on his Hurricane, LK-G, at Exeter.

Flying Officer Watson giving the 'V' for Victory sign before take-off. He survived the war and died in 1986.

Flying Officer Roland Prosper 'Bea' Beamont at Exeter. Destined to become a highly decorated ace and celebrated test pilot, Beamont survived the war. He died in 2001.

Flying Officer William Dennis 'Hurricane' David DFC at Exeter. Another decorated ace and wartime survivor, David passed away in 2000.

Pilot Officer Harry Mitchell was another successful 87 Squadron veteran of the Fall of France and Battle of Britain. A Canadian, he survived the war.

Above: Pictured at Sidmouth, from the left are: 'Rubber'; Flying Officer Tait; Flying Officer Rayner; Flying Officer Watson; Pilot Officer Mallengrau; and Pilot Officer de Spirlet.

Right: Pilot Officer Andrew McLure, a Scot, recorded several Battle of Britain successes, and survived being shot down and wounded, with 87 Squadron – but was sadly killed in a flying accident during 1942; he was twenty-four.

A now famous photograph, snapped by Flying Officer Watson, of 'Widge' leading 'A' Flight on patrol over Bristol during the Battle of Britain.

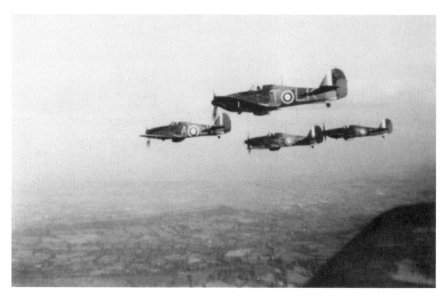

'Widge' leading Flying Officer Ken Tait, Sergeant Howell and Pilot Officer Malengrau.

Another picture showing 'Widge' leading Flying Officer Ken Tait, Sergeant Howell and Pilot Officer Malengrau.

In May 1941, 87 Squadron was sent to operate out of St Mary's, on the Isles of Scilly. Flying Officer Watson and 'Widge' are pictured there after engaging a Ju 88 south of the islands on 28 May 1941.

'Rubber' congratulates the CO on his shared combat success.

No.87 Squadron was now undertaking a significant amount of night operations, the Hurricanes painted matt black.

'Rubber' relaxing at readiness, St Mary's.

'Rubber', phone in hand, 'Larking about at readiness, St Mary's'.

'A' Flight groundcrew – and parrot – with a Hurricane Mk.IIC at St Mary's. Note the fish-tail exhausts and anti-glare panel.

Sergeant Ken Hughes on readiness at St Mary's.

Ken Hughes again, also at St Mary's dispersal.

Squadron Leader 'Widge' Gleed and Flight Lieutenant Roddy Rayner photographed at St Mary's.

'Widge' landing LK-A at St Mary's.

'Rubber' and Hurricane at St Mary's.

'Widge' in Mk IIC Hurricane at St Mary's.

Sergeant Ken Hughes, in 'Mae West', and groundcrew at readiness, St Mary's.

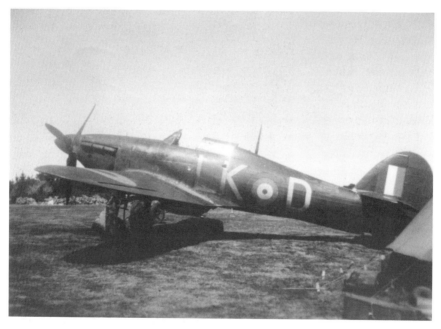

'Rubber's' Mk.IIC, LK-D, at St Mary's.

Above: A Hurricane
Mk.IIC undergoing
maintenance at
St Mary's.

Right: Flight Lieutenant
Peter Roscoe. He was
'killed at Colerne on
night exercise', when
he flew into the ground
near Northleach in
Gloucestershire on
24 February 1942.

Above: Flight Lieutenant Roscoe, with the presentation Hurricane *Agra*.

Left: Flight Lieutenant Roscoe again pictured with a presentation aircraft, this time named *Lucknow*.

Pilot Officer Bill Shimmonds at St Mary's.

'Rubber' and Hurricane, St Mary's.

Flight
Lieutenant
Roddy
Rayner DFC,
St Mary's.

This group photograph has the caption, 'Watson, self, Malengrue, "Widge", Tait, Rayner'. It was taken at Exeter in the autumn of 1940.

Above: The indomitable Irish
Group Captain Victor Beamish
with 'Widge' at St Mary's, 1941.

Right: 'Widge' at St Mary's –
viewed through the Hurricane's
armoured windscreen and
reflector gunsight.

'Rubber', similarly pictured in a rather weathered Hurricane.

A Hurricane pilot's view through the reflector gunsight to the nose-mounted bead-sight.

A number of 87 Squadron's black-painted Hurricane Mk.IIs photographed at Charmy Down during December 1941.

Squadron Leader 'Rubber' Thorogood DFC (right) and friends with a Spitfire graveyard in the Far East, 1945.

Another view of Squadron Leader 'Rubber' Thorogood DFC and friends at the Far East Spitfire graveyard in 1945.

Squadron Leader Thorogood pictured at a Dilip Sarkar book-signing event held at IWM Duxford in 1999.

By 1942, 'Widge' was a Wing Leader, his personal initials, IR-G, adorning his Spitfire.

An official press image of Wing Commander Gleed DSO, DFC, that was released just before he was killed in action.

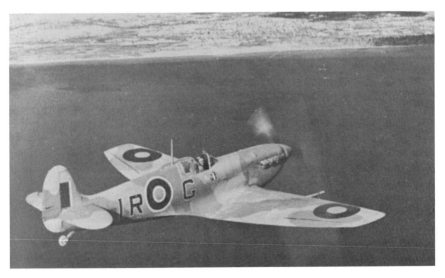

Wing Commander Gleed on patrol over the Tunisian coast – above which he was shot down and killed on 16 April 1943.

Wing Commander Gleed's grave at Enfidaville War Cemetery today. (CWGC, via Kev Barnes).

Bibliography

Adams, P, *Hurricane Squadron: No 87 Squadron at War 1939-41* (Air Research Publications, New Malden, 1988)

Franks, N, *Fighter Leader: The Story of Wing Commander Ian Gleed DSO DFC CdG* (William Kimber, London, 1978)

Sarkar, D, *Hurricane Manual 1940* (Amberley Publishing, Stroud, 2013)

Acknowledgements

I must thank the late Squadron Leader Laurence Thorogood DFC for so kindly providing me copies of his photographs; my friend and publisher, Martin Mace; the team at Pen & Sword, always a pleasure to work with; Andy Long for copying the photographs involved many years ago, and Kev Barnes for organising the photograph of Wing Commander Gleed's grave in Tunisia.

Other Books by Dilip Sarkar

(In order of publication)

Spitfire Squadron: No 19 Squadron at War, 1939-41

The Invisible Thread: A Spitfire's Tale

Through Peril to the Stars: RAF Fighter Pilots Who Failed to Return, 1939-45

Angriff *Westland: Three Battle of Britain Air Raids Through the Looking Glass*

A Few of the Many: Air War 1939-45, A Kaleidoscope of Memories

Bader's Tangmere Spitfires: The Untold Story, 1941

Bader's Duxford Fighters: The Big Wing Controversy

Missing in Action: Resting in Peace?

Guards VC: Blitzkrieg 1940

Battle of Britain: The Photographic Kaleidoscope, Volume I

Battle of Britain: The Photographic Kaleidoscope, Volume II

Battle of Britain: The Photographic Kaleidoscope, Volume III

Battle of Britain: The Photographic Kaleidoscope, Volume IV

Fighter Pilot: The Photographic Kaleidoscope

Group Captain Sir Douglas Bader: An Inspiration in Photographs

Johnnie Johnson: Spitfire Top Gun, Part I

Johnnie Johnson: Spitfire Top Gun, Part II

Battle of Britain: Last Look Back

Spitfire! Courage & Sacrifice

Spitfire Voices: Heroes Remember

The Battle of Powick Bridge: Ambush a Fore-thought

Duxford 1940: A Battle of Britain Base at War

The Few: The Battle of Britain in the Words of the Pilots

Spitfire Manual 1940

The Sinking of HMS Royal Oak: *In the Words of the Survivors (re-print of Hearts of Oak)*

The Last of the Few: Eighteen Battle of Britain Pilots Tell Their Extraordinary Stories

Hearts of Oak: The Human Tragedy of HMS *Royal Oak*

Spitfire Voices: Life as a Spitfire Pilot in the Words of the Veterans

How the Spitfire Won the Battle of Britain

Spitfire Ace of Aces: The True Wartime Story of Johnnie Johnson

Douglas Bader

Fighter Ace: The Extraordinary Life of Douglas Bader, Battle of Britain Hero (re-print of above)

Spitfire: The Photographic Biography

Hurricane Manual 1940

River Pike

The Final Few: The Last Surviving Pilots of the Battle of Britain Tell Their Stories

Arnhem 1944: The Human Tragedy of the Bridge Too Far

Spitfire! The Full Story of a Unique Battle of Britain Fighter Squadron

Battle of Britain 1940: The Finest Hour's Human Cost

Letters From The Few: Unique Memories of the Battle of Britain

Johnnie Johnson's 1942 Diary: The War Diary of the Spitfire Ace of Aces (Ed)

Johnnie Johnson's Great Adventure: The Spitfire Ace of Ace's Last Look Back (Ed)

Spitfire Ace of Aces: The Photographs of Johnnie Johnson

Sailor Malan – Freedom Fighter: The Inspirational Story of a Spitfire Ace

The Real Spitfire Pilot: Flight Lieutenant DM Crook DFC's Original Unpublished Manuscript (Ed)

Bader's Big Wing Controversy, Duxford 1940